Q-90 TEST YOUR KNOWLED

THIS IS YOUR **PASSBOOK®** FOR ...

ORAL PATHOLOGY/ RADIOGRAPHY

NLC®

NATIONAL LEARNING CORPORATION®

passbooks.com

NLC®

National Learning Corporation

212 Michael Drive, Syosset, NY 11791
(516) 921-8888 • www.passbooks.com
E-mail: info@passbooks.com

PUBLISHED IN THE UNITED STATES OF AMERICA

PASSBOOK® SERIES

THE *PASSBOOK® SERIES* has been created to prepare applicants and candidates for the ultimate academic battlefield – the examination room.

At some time in our lives, each and every one of us may be required to take an examination – for validation, matriculation, admission, qualification, registration, certification, or licensure.

Based on the assumption that every applicant or candidate has met the basic formal educational standards, has taken the required number of courses, and read the necessary texts, the *PASSBOOK® SERIES* furnishes the one special preparation which may assure passing with confidence, instead of failing with insecurity. Examination questions – together with answers – are furnished as the basic vehicle for study so that the mysteries of the examination and its compounding difficulties may be eliminated or diminished by a sure method.

This book is meant to help you pass your examination provided that you qualify and are serious in your objective.

The entire field is reviewed through the huge store of content information which is succinctly presented through a provocative and challenging approach – the question-and-answer method.

A climate of success is established by furnishing the correct answers at the end of each test.

You soon learn to recognize types of questions, forms of questions, and patterns of questioning. You may even begin to anticipate expected outcomes.

You perceive that many questions are repeated or adapted so that you can gain acute insights, which may enable you to score many sure points.

You learn how to confront new questions, or types of questions, and to attack them confidently and work out the correct answers.

You note objectives and emphases, and recognize pitfalls and dangers, so that you may make positive educational adjustments.

Moreover, you are kept fully informed in relation to new concepts, methods, practices, and directions in the field.

You discover that you arre actually taking the examination all the time: you are preparing for the examination by "taking" an examination, not by reading extraneous and/or supererogatory textbooks.

In short, this PASSBOOK®, used directedly, should be an important factor in helping you to pass your test.

HOW TO TAKE A TEST

You have studied long, hard and conscientiously.

With your official admission card in hand, and your heart pounding, you have been admitted to the examination room.

You note that there are several hundred other applicants in the examination room waiting to take the same test.

They all appear to be equally well prepared.

You know that nothing but your best effort will suffice. The "moment of truth" is at hand: you now have to demonstrate objectively, in writing, your knowledge of content and your understanding of subject matter.

You are fighting the most important battle of your life—to pass and/or score high on an examination which will determine your career and provide the economic basis for your livelihood.

What extra, special things should you know and should you do in taking the examination?

I. YOU MUST PASS AN EXAMINATION

A. WHAT EVERY CANDIDATE SHOULD KNOW

Examination applicants often ask us for help in preparing for the written test. What can I study in advance? What kinds of questions will be asked? How will the test be given? How will the papers be graded?

B. HOW ARE EXAMS DEVELOPED?

Examinations are carefully written by trained technicians who are specialists in the field known as "psychological measurement," in consultation with recognized authorities in the field of work that the test will cover. These experts recommend the subject matter areas or skills to be tested; only those knowledges or skills important to your success on the job are included. The most reliable books and source materials available are used as references. Together, the experts and technicians judge the difficulty level of the questions.

Test technicians know how to phrase questions so that the problem is clearly stated. Their ethics do not permit "trick" or "catch" questions. Questions may have been tried out on sample groups, or subjected to statistical analysis, to determine their usefulness.

Written tests are often used in combination with performance tests, ratings of training and experience, and oral interviews. All of these measures combine to form the best-known means of finding the right person for the right job.

II. HOW TO PASS THE WRITTEN TEST

A. BASIC STEPS

1) Study the announcement

How, then, can you know what subjects to study? Our best answer is: "Learn as much as possible about the class of positions for which you've applied." The exam will test the knowledge, skills and abilities needed to do the work.

Your most valuable source of information about the position you want is the official exam announcement. This announcement lists the training and experience qualifications. Check these standards and apply only if you come reasonably close to meeting them. Many jurisdictions preview the written test in the exam announcement by including a section called "Knowledge and Abilities Required," "Scope of the Examination," or some similar heading. Here you will find out specifically what fields will be tested.

2) Choose appropriate study materials

If the position for which you are applying is technical or advanced, you will read more advanced, specialized material. If you are already familiar with the basic principles of your field, elementary textbooks would waste your time. Concentrate on advanced textbooks and technical periodicals. Think through the concepts and review difficult problems in your field.

These are all general sources. You can get more ideas on your own initiative, following these leads. For example, training manuals and publications of the government agency which employs workers in your field can be useful, particularly for technical and professional positions. A letter or visit to the government department involved may result in more specific study suggestions, and certainly will provide you with a more definite idea of the exact nature of the position you are seeking.

3) Study this book!

III. KINDS OF TESTS

Tests are used for purposes other than measuring knowledge and ability to perform specified duties. For some positions, it is equally important to test ability to make adjustments to new situations or to profit from training. In others, basic mental abilities not dependent on information are essential. Questions which test these things may not appear as pertinent to the duties of the position as those which test for knowledge and information. Yet they are often highly important parts of a fair examination. For very general questions, it is almost impossible to help you direct your study efforts. What we can do is to point out some of the more common of these general abilities needed in public service positions and describe some typical questions.

1) General information

Broad, general information has been found useful for predicting job success in some kinds of work. This is tested in a variety of ways, from vocabulary lists to questions about current events. Basic background in some field of work, such as sociology or economics, may be sampled in a group of questions. Often these are principles which have become familiar to most persons through exposure rather than through formal training. It is difficult to advise you how to study for these questions; being alert to the world around you is our best suggestion.

2) Verbal ability

An example of an ability needed in many positions is verbal or language ability. Verbal ability is, in brief, the ability to use and understand words. Vocabulary and grammar tests are typical measures of this ability. Reading comprehension or paragraph interpretation questions are common in many kinds of civil service tests. You are given a paragraph of written material and asked to find its central meaning.

IV. KINDS OF QUESTIONS

1. Multiple-choice Questions

Most popular of the short-answer questions is the "multiple choice" or "best answer" question. It can be used, for example, to test for factual knowledge, ability to solve problems or judgment in meeting situations found at work.

A multiple-choice question is normally one of three types:

- It can begin with an incomplete statement followed by several possible endings. You are to find the one ending which *best* completes the statement, although some of the others may not be entirely wrong.
- It can also be a complete statement in the form of a question which is answered by choosing one of the statements listed.
- It can be in the form of a problem – again you select the best answer.

Here is an example of a multiple-choice question with a discussion which should give you some clues as to the method for choosing the right answer:

When an employee has a complaint about his assignment, the action which will *best* help him overcome his difficulty is to

A. discuss his difficulty with his coworkers
B. take the problem to the head of the organization
C. take the problem to the person who gave him the assignment
D. say nothing to anyone about his complaint

In answering this question, you should study each of the choices to find which is best. Consider choice "A" – Certainly an employee may discuss his complaint with fellow employees, but no change or improvement can result, and the complaint remains unresolved. Choice "B" is a poor choice since the head of the organization probably does not know what assignment you have been given, and taking your problem to him is known as "going over the head" of the supervisor. The supervisor, or person who made the assignment, is the person who can clarify it or correct any injustice. Choice "C" is, therefore, correct. To say nothing, as in choice "D," is unwise. Supervisors have and interest in knowing the problems employees are facing, and the employee is seeking a solution to his problem.

2. True/False

3. Matching Questions

Matching an answer from a column of choices within another column.

V. RECORDING YOUR ANSWERS

Computer terminals are used more and more today for many different kinds of exams.

For an examination with very few applicants, you may be told to record your answers in the test booklet itself. Separate answer sheets are much more common. If this separate answer sheet is to be scored by machine – and this is often the case – it is highly important that you mark your answers correctly in order to get credit.

VI. BEFORE THE TEST

YOUR PHYSICAL CONDITION IS IMPORTANT

If you are not well, you can't do your best work on tests. If you are half asleep, you can't do your best either. Here are some tips:

1) Get about the same amount of sleep you usually get. Don't stay up all night before the test, either partying or worrying—DON'T DO IT!
2) If you wear glasses, be sure to wear them when you go to take the test. This goes for hearing aids, too.
3) If you have any physical problems that may keep you from doing your best, be sure to tell the person giving the test. If you are sick or in poor health, you relay cannot do your best on any test. You can always come back and take the test some other time.

Common sense will help you find procedures to follow to get ready for an examination. Too many of us, however, overlook these sensible measures. Indeed, nervousness and fatigue have been found to be the most serious reasons why applicants fail to do their best on civil service tests. Here is a list of reminders:

- Begin your preparation early – Don't wait until the last minute to go scurrying around for books and materials or to find out what the position is all about.
- Prepare continuously – An hour a night for a week is better than an all-night cram session. This has been definitely established. What is more, a night a week for a month will return better dividends than crowding your study into a shorter period of time.
- Locate the place of the exam – You have been sent a notice telling you when and where to report for the examination. If the location is in a different town or otherwise unfamiliar to you, it would be well to inquire the best route and learn something about the building.
- Relax the night before the test – Allow your mind to rest. Do not study at all that night. Plan some mild recreation or diversion; then go to bed early and get a good night's sleep.
- Get up early enough to make a leisurely trip to the place for the test – This way unforeseen events, traffic snarls, unfamiliar buildings, etc. will not upset you.

- Dress comfortably – A written test is not a fashion show. You will be known by number and not by name, so wear something comfortable.
- Leave excess paraphernalia at home – Shopping bags and odd bundles will get in your way. You need bring only the items mentioned in the official notice you received; usually everything you need is provided. Do not bring reference books to the exam. They will only confuse those last minutes and be taken away from you when in the test room.
- Arrive somewhat ahead of time – If because of transportation schedules you must get there very early, bring a newspaper or magazine to take your mind off yourself while waiting.
- Locate the examination room – When you have found the proper room, you will be directed to the seat or part of the room where you will sit. Sometimes you are given a sheet of instructions to read while you are waiting. Do not fill out any forms until you are told to do so; just read them and be prepared.
- Relax and prepare to listen to the instructions
- If you have any physical problem that may keep you from doing your best, be sure to tell the test administrator. If you are sick or in poor health, you really cannot do your best on the exam. You can come back and take the test some other time.

VII. AT THE TEST

The day of the test is here and you have the test booklet in your hand. The temptation to get going is very strong. Caution! There is more to success than knowing the right answers. You must know how to identify your papers and understand variations in the type of short-answer question used in this particular examination. Follow these suggestions for maximum results from your efforts:

1) Cooperate with the monitor

The test administrator has a duty to create a situation in which you can be as much at ease as possible. He will give instructions, tell you when to begin, check to see that you are marking your answer sheet correctly, and so on. He is not there to guard you, although he will see that your competitors do not take unfair advantage. He wants to help you do your best.

2) Listen to all instructions

Don't jump the gun! Wait until you understand all directions. In most civil service tests you get more time than you need to answer the questions. So don't be in a hurry. Read each word of instructions until you clearly understand the meaning. Study the examples, listen to all announcements and follow directions. Ask questions if you do not understand what to do.

3) Identify your papers

Civil service exams are usually identified by number only. You will be assigned a number; you must not put your name on your test papers. Be sure to copy your number correctly. Since more than one exam may be given, copy your exact examination title.

4) Plan your time

Unless you are told that a test is a "speed" or "rate of work" test, speed itself is usually not important. Time enough to answer all the questions will be provided, but this does not mean that you have all day. An overall time limit has been set. Divide the total time (in minutes) by the number of questions to determine the approximate time you have for each question.

5) Do not linger over difficult questions

If you come across a difficult question, mark it with a paper clip (useful to have along) and come back to it when you have been through the booklet. One caution if you do this – be sure to skip a number on your answer sheet as well. Check often to be sure that you have not lost your place and that you are marking in the row numbered the same as the question you are answering.

6) Read the questions

Be sure you know what the question asks! Many capable people are unsuccessful because they failed to *read* the questions correctly.

7) Answer all questions

Unless you have been instructed that a penalty will be deducted for incorrect answers, it is better to guess than to omit a question.

8) Speed tests

It is often better NOT to guess on speed tests. It has been found that on timed tests people are tempted to spend the last few seconds before time is called in marking answers at random – without even reading them – in the hope of picking up a few extra points. To discourage this practice, the instructions may warn you that your score will be "corrected" for guessing. That is, a penalty will be applied. The incorrect answers will be deducted from the correct ones, or some other penalty formula will be used.

9) Review your answers

If you finish before time is called, go back to the questions you guessed or omitted to give them further thought. Review other answers if you have time.

10) Return your test materials

If you are ready to leave before others have finished or time is called, take ALL your materials to the monitor and leave quietly. Never take any test material with you. The monitor can discover whose papers are not complete, and taking a test booklet may be grounds for disqualification.

VIII. EXAMINATION TECHNIQUES

1) Read the general instructions carefully. These are usually printed on the first page of the exam booklet. As a rule, these instructions refer to the timing of the examination; the fact that you should not start work until the signal and must stop work at a signal, etc. If there are any *special* instructions, such as a choice of questions to be answered, make sure that you note this instruction carefully.

2) When you are ready to start work on the examination, that is as soon as the signal has been given, read the instructions to each question booklet, underline any key words or phrases, such as *least*, *best*, *outline*, *describe*

and the like. In this way you will tend to answer as requested rather than discover on reviewing your paper that you *listed without describing*, that you selected the *worst* choice rather than the *best* choice, etc.

3) If the examination is of the objective or multiple-choice type – that is, each question will also give a series of possible answers: A, B, C or D, and you are called upon to select the best answer and write the letter next to that answer on your answer paper – it is advisable to start answering each question in turn. There may be anywhere from 50 to 100 such questions in the three or four hours allotted and you can see how much time would be taken if you read through all the questions before beginning to answer any. Furthermore, if you come across a question or group of questions which you know would be difficult to answer, it would undoubtedly affect your handling of all the other questions.

4) If the examination is of the essay type and contains but a few questions, it is a moot point as to whether you should read all the questions before starting to answer any one. Of course, if you are given a choice – say five out of seven and the like – then it is essential to read all the questions so you can eliminate the two that are most difficult. If, however, you are asked to answer all the questions, there may be danger in trying to answer the easiest one first because you may find that you will spend too much time on it. The best technique is to answer the first question, then proceed to the second, etc.

5) Time your answers. Before the exam begins, write down the time it started, then add the time allowed for the examination and write down the time it must be completed, then divide the time available somewhat as follows:
   - If 3-1/2 hours are allowed, that would be 210 minutes. If you have 80 objective-type questions, that would be an average of 2-1/2 minutes per question. Allow yourself no more than 2 minutes per question, or a total of 160 minutes, which will permit about 50 minutes to review.
   - If for the time allotment of 210 minutes there are 7 essay questions to answer, that would average about 30 minutes a question. Give yourself only 25 minutes per question so that you have about 35 minutes to review.

6) The most important instruction is to *read each question* and make sure you know what is wanted. The second most important instruction is to *time yourself properly* so that you answer every question. The third most important instruction is to *answer every question*. Guess if you have to but include something for each question. Remember that you will receive no credit for a blank and will probably receive some credit if you write something in answer to an essay question. If you guess a letter – say "B" for a multiple-choice question – you may have guessed right. If you leave a blank as an answer to a multiple-choice question, the examiners may respect your feelings but it will not add a point to your score. Some exams may penalize you for wrong answers, so in such cases *only*, you may not want to guess unless you have some basis for your answer.

7) Suggestions
   a. Objective-type questions
      1. Examine the question booklet for proper sequence of pages and questions
      2. Read all instructions carefully
      3. Skip any question which seems too difficult; return to it after all other questions have been answered
      4. Apportion your time properly; do not spend too much time on any single question or group of questions
      5. Note and underline key words – *all, most, fewest, least, best, worst, same, opposite,* etc.
      6. Pay particular attention to negatives
      7. Note unusual option, e.g., unduly long, short, complex, different or similar in content to the body of the question
      8. Observe the use of "hedging" words – *probably, may, most likely,* etc.
      9. Make sure that your answer is put next to the same number as the question
      10. Do not second-guess unless you have good reason to believe the second answer is definitely more correct
      11. Cross out original answer if you decide another answer is more accurate; do not erase until you are ready to hand your paper in
      12. Answer all questions; guess unless instructed otherwise
      13. Leave time for review

   b. Essay questions
      1. Read each question carefully
      2. Determine exactly what is wanted. Underline key words or phrases.
      3. Decide on outline or paragraph answer
      4. Include many different points and elements unless asked to develop any one or two points or elements
      5. Show impartiality by giving pros and cons unless directed to select one side only
      6. Make and write down any assumptions you find necessary to answer the questions
      7. Watch your English, grammar, punctuation and choice of words
      8. Time your answers; don't crowd material

8) Answering the essay question

Most essay questions can be answered by framing the specific response around several key words or ideas. Here are a few such key words or ideas:

M's: manpower, materials, methods, money, management
P's: purpose, program, policy, plan, procedure, practice, problems, pitfalls, personnel, public relations

a. Six basic steps in handling problems:
   1. Preliminary plan and background development
   2. Collect information, data and facts
   3. Analyze and interpret information, data and facts
   4. Analyze and develop solutions as well as make recommendations

5. Prepare report and sell recommendations
6. Install recommendations and follow up effectiveness

b. Pitfalls to avoid

1. *Taking things for granted* – A statement of the situation does not necessarily imply that each of the elements is necessarily true; for example, a complaint may be invalid and biased so that all that can be taken for granted is that a complaint has been registered
2. *Considering only one side of a situation* – Wherever possible, indicate several alternatives and then point out the reasons you selected the best one
3. *Failing to indicate follow up* – Whenever your answer indicates action on your part, make certain that you will take proper follow-up action to see how successful your recommendations, procedures or actions turn out to be
4. *Taking too long in answering any single question* – Remember to time your answers properly

EXAMINATION SECTION

ORAL PATHOLOGY / RADIOGRAPHY

EXAMINATION SECTION
TEST 1

DIRECTIONS: Each question or incomplete statement is followed by several suggested answers or completions. Select the one that BEST answers the question or completes the statement. *PRINT THE LETTER OF THE CORRECT ANSWER IN THE SPACE AT THE RIGHT.*

1. Hand-foot-mouth disease is caused by 1.____
   A. emotional stress
   B. strains of varicella virus
   C. strains of Coxsackie virus A
   D. strains of streptococcus mutans
   E. allergy to cats or other domestic animals

2. The quality of an x-ray beam can be MOST accurately described by 2.____
   A. kilovoltage
   B. milliamperage
   C. exposure time
   D. half-value layer

3. Ludwig's angina is an infection MOST commonly relate to 3.____
   A. maxillary molars
   B. mandibular molars
   C. maxillary premolars
   D. maxillary anterior teeth
   E. mandibular anterior teeth

4. Multiple discrete apical radiolucencies associated with vital asymptomatic mandibular teeth is MOST suggestive of 4.____
   A. periapical cysts
   B. dental granulomas
   C. immature cementomas
   D. non-odontogenic cysts
   E. chronic dento-alveolar abscesses

5. A 16-year-old girl has a slowly progressive enlargement of the left side of the mandible, of 18 months duration. Radiographic examination reveals the replacement of the normal trabecular pattern by a poorly circumscribed multilocular radiolucency. The developing third molar has been displaced into the ramus. Biopsy of the lesional tissue reveals it to be composed of a relatively afibrillar, faintly staining ground substance, infrequently scattered throughout which are small spindle-shaped cells. These have small deeply staining nuclei and delicate cytoplasmic projections. 5.____
   The diagnosis MOST consistent with these changes is
   A. ameloblastoma
   B. myxoma of bone
   C. osteogenic sarcoma
   D. aneurysmal bone cyst
   E. juvenile ossifying fibroma

6. Following a momentary constriction of the blood vessels, the first vascular response to injury in the sequence of events in inflammation is 6.____
   A. margination of leukocytes
   B. dilatation of blood vessels
   C. diapedesis of leukocytes
   D. phagocytosis of bacteria or other foreign particles
   E. exudation of serum proteins

7. Dilaceration is the severe angular distortion of a tooth which generally involves the roots and is the result of 7.____
   A. trauma B. heredity C. malnutrition D. decalcification

8. Pernicious anemia is USUALLY associated with 8.____
   A. glossitis B. blue sclera
   C. iron deficiency D. microcytic anemia
   E. gastric hyperacidity

9. Taurodontism is a term applied to teeth which 9.____
   A. have large pulp chambers and relatively short roots
   B. are rotated in the dental arch
   C. are congenitally displaced lingually
   D. have multiple supernumerary cusps, congenitally

10. Proliferation of multinucleated giant cells, histiocytes, fibroblasts, and capillaries occurring about a fragment of suture material embedded in the oral mucosa is called 10.____
   A. cicatrix B. cellulitis
   C. pyogenic granuloma D. giant cell granuloma
   E. foreign body granuloma

11. The mucocele is a lesion MOST likely formed as a result of 11.____
   A. rupture of the salivary duct
   B. partial or complete compression of the salivary acini
   C. inflammatory changes in the glandular interstitial tissue
   D. partial or complete obstruction of the salivary duct by calculus

12. The wavelength of x-rays is determined by the 12.____
   A. kilovoltage
   B. milliamperage
   C. voltage in the filament circuit
   D. quantity of electrons in the cathode system

13. Hypophosphatasia is a hereditary error of metabolism. When manifested in children, the MOST common finding is 13.____
   A. delayed eruption
   B. generalized ankyloses
   C. hypercementosis
   D. supernumerary teeth
   E. early exfoliation of anterior deciduous teeth

14. The PRINCIPAL difference between rheumatoid arthritis and osteoarthritis of the temporomandibular joint is that rheumatoid arthritis 14.____
   A. is thought to be caused by abnormal function or senility changes, whereas osteoarthritis is thought to be an auto-immune disease
   B. responds to aspirin therapy only, whereas osteoarthritis responds to cortisone therapy only
   C. is thought to be an auto-immune disease, whereas osteoarthritis is thought to be caused by senile functional changes
   D. can be treated medically with rest, heat, and cortisone, whereas osteoarthritis always requires osteotomy with arthroplasty

15. Severe pain which arises following sectioning or injury to a peripheral nerve and which may occur following tooth extraction is CHARACTERISTIC of 15.____
   A. causalgia
   B. Horner's syndrome
   C. Meniere's disease
   D. myasthenia gravis
   E. auriculotemporal syndrome

16. Sharpness of the radiographic image is INCREASED by 16.____
   A. using a smaller focal spot-object distance
   B. decreasing the focal spot-object distance
   C. decreasing the milliamperage
   D. increasing the object-film distance

17. Recurrence after surgical removal is a noteworthy feature of the pleomorphic adenoma of the salivary glands. 17.____
   The factor considered MOST responsible for this is the
   A. tendency to infiltrate the capsule
   B. marked and early lymph node involvement
   C. proven multicentric origin of the tumor
   D. anaplastic histologic characteristics of the tumor
   E. tendency of the tumor to show hematogenous metastases

18. Primary and secondary dentin are ALIKE in the 18.____
   A. course and number of the dentinal tubules
   B. regularity and pattern of the dentinal tubules
   C. degree of mineralization of the dentin
   D. type of cell necessary for formation of the dentin

19. Cherubism is GENERALLY considered to be a familiar type of 19.____
   A. osteitis fibrosa cystica
   B. osteogenesis imperfecta
   C. osteítis deformans
   D. osteopetrosis
   E. none of the above

20. A patient, age 45, has pain in the jaw. On radiographs of the jaw, several small, regular, distinct, radiolucent lesions are seen. The laboratory tests show Bence Jones protein in the urine. 20.____
   The patient PROBABLY has
   A. fibrosarcoma
   B. osteosarcoma
   C. multiple myeloma
   D. metastatic carcinoma

21. A patient 16 years of age has delayed eruption of permanent teeth and prolonged retention of deciduous teeth. Radiographs indicate multiple impactions of the unerupted permanent teeth. Head size appears large with prominent frontal bossae and slightly constricted facial features. Diagnosis suggested is 21.____
    A. congenital syphilis
    B. ectodermal dysplasia
    C. osteogenesis imperfecta
    D. cleidocranial dysostosis
    E. dentinogenesis imperfecta

22. *Burning tongue* may be a symptom of 22.____
    A. pernicious anemia
    B. xerostomia
    C. vitamin B complex deficiency
    D. all of the above

23. Progressive increase in mandibular length and in mandibular interdental spacing in an adult patient is characteristic of 23.____
    A. periodontosis
    B. hypothyroidism
    C. hyperpituitarism
    D. Addison's disease
    E. hyperparathyroidism

24. Chronic hyperplastic pulpitis occurs CHIEFLY in 24.____
    A. older individuals with fibrosed pulps
    B. teeth with large metallic restorations
    C. children and young adults with large open cavities
    D. molar teeth with relatively small carious lesions

25. If a single developing permanent tooth bud is damaged so that the tooth erupts with defective enamel, this condition is described as 25.____
    A. mesiodens
    B. partial anodontia
    C. Hutchinson's tooth
    D. Turner tooth

KEY (CORRECT ANSWERS)

1.	C	11.	A
2.	D	12.	A
3.	B	13.	E
4.	C	14.	C
5.	B	15.	A
6.	B	16.	A
7.	A	17.	A
8.	A	18.	D
9.	A	19.	E
10.	E	20.	C

21.	D
22.	D
23.	C
24.	C
25.	D

TEST 2

DIRECTIONS: Each question or incomplete statement is followed by several suggested answers or completions. Select the one that BEST answers the question or completes the statement. *PRINT THE LETTER OF THE CORRECT ANSWER IN THE SPACE AT THE RIGHT.*

1. If the progress of a carious lesion has advanced far enough to cause an early inflammatory reaction in the pulp, one would USUALLY expect 1.____
   A. hemorrhage
   B. apical infection
   C. pulpal fibrosis
   D. no bacteria in the pulp
   E. many bacteria in the pulp

2. Each of the following clinical and microscopic changes is characteristic of solar cheilitis EXCEPT 2.____
   A. hyperkeratosis
   B. multinucleated giant cells
   C. atrophy of the vermilion border of the lip
   D. basophilic degeneration of collagen
   E. loss of definition of the mucocutaneous junction of the lip

3. A 39-year-old woman has periodic episodes of mild ill-defined pain referable to the right maxillary central incisor. Section prepared from the extracted tooth revealed replacement of the normal coronal pulp by a very cellular connective tissue. The odontoblastic layer in the coronal pulp was absent. The dentin was reduced in thickness, and the pulpal margin of the dentin was irregularly scalloped, with multinucleated giant cells, identified in juxtaposition to the scalloped border. 3.____
   The diagnosis MOST consistent with these changes is
   A. hyperparathyroidism
   B. recticular atrophy of pulp
   C. chronic hyperplastic pulpitis
   D. hereditary dentinogenesis imperfecta
   E. pulpal hyperplasia with idiopathic resorption

4. Multiple myeloma is often associated with all of the following EXCEPT 4.____
   A. bone pain
   B. Bence Jones proteinuria
   C. osteoblastic bone lesions
   D. myeloma cells in bone marrow

5. A pulpal condition in which there are masses of bacteria in the decayed dentin near the pulp, no bacteria in the pulp, a serous and polymorphonuclear cellular exudate in a pulp horn is MOST likely 5.____
   A. chronic partial pulpitis
   B. acute partial pulpitis
   C. hyperplastic pulpitis
   D. hyperemia

6. All of the following anatomic structures are usually recognized on intra-oral periapical radiographs EXCEPT 6.____
   A. mental foramen
   B. mylohyoid ridge
   C. coronoid process
   D. pterygoid Hamulus
   E. mandibular foramen
   F. median palatine suture

7. The gummy substance which facilitates plaque adherence to the tooth surface is produced by bacterial conversion of a carbohydrate to 7.____
   A. dextran
   B. glucose
   C. sucrose
   D. glycogen
   E. dextranase

8. Numerous areas of radiolucency in bones are common to each of the following EXCEPT 8.____
   A. multiple myeloma
   B. hyperparathyroidism
   C. Albers-Schönbert disease
   D. metastatic tumors of bone
   E. Hand-Schüller Christian disease

9. Which of the following terms is used to define a developmental fault in which there is an overgrowth of tissue native to the area? 9.____
   A. Teratoma
   B. Chloroma
   C. Harmartoma
   D. Choristoma
   E. Chemodectoma

10. An acute infectious inflammatory condition is characterized initially by small, elevated, round or oval vesicles 2 to 5 mm. in diameter, which appear either singly or in groups on the inner surface of the lips, cheeks, gingiva, and tongue. The vesicles rupture within hours leaving small superficial ulcers bordered by red margins. 10.____
    This is suggestive of
    A. herpetic gingivostomatitis
    B. infectious mononucleosis
    C. streptococcic stomatitis
    D. bullous lichen planus
    E. erythema multiforme

11. Which of the following conditions is MOST suspect if a radiograph shows a dense, diffuse radiopacity at the apex of a mandibular left first molar having a filled root canal and widening of the periodontal space at the apex of the mesial root? 11.____
    A. Osteoma
    B Cementoma
    C. Dental granuloma
    D. Sclerosing osteitis

12. Yellow-brown stained radiographs are the result of 12.____
    A. old films
    B. exhausted solutions
    C. insufficient washing
    D. improper temperature of developing solution

13. A 19-year-old patient shows a relatively large spherical radiolucency in the left third molar region of the mandible. The patient has a full complement of posterior teeth with the exception of the mandibular left third molar. The patient says he never had a *wisdom tooth* on that side. 13.____

Although a definitive diagnosis cannot be made on the basis of radiographic evidence alone, which of the following is suggested? _____ cyst.
A. Periodontal (dentoperiosteal type)
B. Extravasation
C. Primordial
D. Dermoid

14. A patient exhibits a unilateral, slowly progressive elongation of the face with deviation of the chin away from the affected side. The condyle shows clinical and radiographic evidence of enlargement. Severe malocclusion is evident. The condition described is 14.____
A. subluxation
B. Costen's syndrome
C. aplasia of condyle
D. hyperplasia of condyle

15. Which of the following has been determined to be the MOST cariogenic carbohydrate? 15.____
A. Starch
B. Sucrose
C. Glucose
D. Glycogen
E. Dextranase
F. All are sugars and thus equally cariogenic

16. Erythroblastosis fetalis may be a cause of 16.____
A. blue sclera
B. pigmented teeth
C. Fordyce's granules
D. peg lateral incisors
E. supernumerary incisors

17. Which of the following dental conditions is common to cleidocranial dysostosis, hypopituitarism, and rickets? 17.____
A. Delayed eruption of teeth
B. Missing or malformed clavicles
C. Microdontia
D. Enamel hypoplasia

18. A distinct clinical entity originating as a proliferative response of tissues to a nonspecific infection or irritation is called 18.____
A. abscess
B. cellulitis
C. canker sores
D. pyogenic granuloma
E. all of the above

19. An ameloblastoma may be classified as a(n) _____ tumor. 19.____
A. mesodermal odontogenic
B. mesodermal nonodontogenic
C. ectodermal odontogenic
D. ectodermal nonodontogenic
E. mixed (ectodermal and mesodermal) odontogenic

20. A seven-year-old girl has a temperature of 102°F. Her mother states that the child has had an upper respiratory infection for several days. Examination reveals a few small white dots surrounded by a reddish halo on the buccal mucosa. 20.____
The oral lesions MOST probably are indicative of
A. rubeola
B. herpangina
C. varicella
D. herpes zoster
E. hand-foot-mouth disease

21. In an illustration where, in the diagram, *a* points on the upper left side to a film holder, *b*, which is directly to the right, PROBABLY represents 21.____
A. adumbration
B calculus
C. exostosis
D. cementoma

22. In the illustration referred to in Question 21, *c*, at the center, bottom, PROBABLY represents 22.____
A. an exostosis
B. an impacted premolar
C. sclerotic bone
D. a cementoma
E. a supernumerary tooth

23. Which of the following is LEAST effective in reducing patient radiation dose? 23.____
A. Fast films
B. Higher kilovoltage
C. Proper collimation
D. Increased filtration

24. Xerostomia is LEAST likely to occur in which of the following? 24.____
A. Atropine administration
B. Chronic sialadenitis
C. Vitamin C deficiency
D. Antihistamine administration
E. Sjögren's syndrome

25. The reason for adding an aluminum disk in the primary x-ray beam is to 25.____
A. reduce exposure time
B. reduce long wavelength radiation
C. permit the use of faster film
D. increase density of exposed film
E. reduce the diameter of the primary beam

KEY (CORRECT ANSWERS)

1. B
2. B
3. E
4. C
5. B

6. E
7. A
8. C
9. C
10. A

11. D
12. C
13. C
14. D
15. B

16. B
17. A
18. D
19. C
20. A

21. B
22. A
23. B
24. C
25. B

ORAL PATHOLOGY / RADIOGRAPHY

EXAMINATION SECTION
TEST 1

DIRECTIONS: Each question or incomplete statement is followed by several suggested answers or completions. Select the one that BEST answers the question or completes the statement. *PRINT THE LETTER OF THE CORRECT ANSWER IN THE SPACE AT THE RIGHT.*

1. Acute leukemia may be characterized by which of the following? 1.____

   A. Anemia
   B. Thrombocytopenia
   C. Prolonged bleeding time
   D. Elevated leukocyte count
   E. All of the above

2. Radiographs of a young adult show that all permanent teeth have small roots and obliterated pulp chambers. 2.____
   These findings are indicative of

   A. osteomalacia
   B. amelogenesis imperfecta
   C. cleidocranial dysostosis
   D. dentinogenesis imperfecta
   E. none of the above

3. Which of the following diseases is characterized by normal serum calcium and phosphorus and elevated serum alkaline phosphatase? 3.____

   A. Osteomalacia
   B. Renal rickets
   C. Paget's disease
   D. Hypoparathyroidism
   E. Hyperparathyroidism

4. Aspiration of blood or fragments of tissue during operative procedures in the mouth MOST frequently results in 4.____

   A. fatal laryngeal spasm
   B. lobar pneumonia
   C. laryngitis
   D. lung abscess
   E. actinomycosis of the lung

5. Of the following, which is a MAJOR neuralgia that may be characterized as a paroxysmal disturbance of the fifth cranial nerve and the presence of a *trigger zone?* 5.____

   A. Trigeminal neuralgia
   B. Orolingual paresthesia
   C. Sphenopalatine neuralgia
   D. Glossopharyngeal neuralgia
   E. None of the above

6. An 18-year-old man complains of a painful swelling in the palate. Examination reveals a soft, fluctuant, tender mass in the midline of the hard palate. The teeth test vital, and there is no evidence of periodontal disease. Radiographs, however, reveal a well-defined radiolucency between the roots of the maxillary central incisors. 6.____
The clinical and radiographic findings are compatible with the diagnosis of a _______ cyst.

A. lateral periodontal
B. globulomaxillary
C. incisive canal
D. nasoalveolar
E. none of the above

7. Which of the following connective tissue tumors is noted for the property of inducing pseudocarcinomatous change in adjacent epithelium? 7.____

A. Fibroma
B. Neurilemoma
C. Fibrosarcoma
D. Granular cell myoblastoma
E. None of the above

8. The rarefaction occurring in the bone from an infected deciduous molar, as studied radiographically, MOST frequently appears 8.____

A. about the apices
B. between two teeth
C. in the bifurcation
D. around the developing permanent tooth
E. as a uniform widening of the periodontal ligament space

9. Which of the following is MOST characteristic of cervico-facial actinomycosis? 9.____

A. Single or multiple ulcers
B. Enlarged cervical lymph nodes
C. Multiple abscesses with sinuses
D. Indurated nodules in the skin of the neck
E. Incrustation of the skin of the cheek and neck

10. Fordyce's granules appear microscopically to be 10.____

A. sweat glands
B. sebaceous glands
C. actinomycotic lesions
D. mucous salivary glands
E. serous salivary glands

11. Which of the following experimental data would substantiate the important role of bacteria in the etiology of dental caries? 11.____

A. Lactobacillus acidophilus is found in higher concentrations in the mouths of patients with rampant caries.
B. Dental caries does not develop in susceptible experimental animals born and raised in a germ-free environment.
C. Acidity of dental plaque can drop below a pH of 5.0.
D. All of the above
E. None of the above

12. Which of the following anatomic structures appear as radiopacities in periapical radiographs? 12.____

I. Nasal septum
II. Anterior nasal spine
III. Genial tubercles
IV. Submandibular gland fossa
V. Mylohyoid ridge
VI. Mental foramen
VII. Median suture

The CORRECT answer is:

A. I, II, III, IV
B. IV, V, VI, VII
C. I, II, III, V
D. I, III, VI, VII
E. III, IV, V, VI

13. Which of the following statements concerning the dental granuloma is NOT true? They 13.____

A. are associated with vital teeth
B. are radiolucent on radiographs
C. may contain cholesterol crystals
D. may develop into a cyst
E. are often asymptomatic

14. Which of the following would be considered in the differential diagnosis of a well-defined radiolucency at the apex of an endodontically treated tooth with a history of periapical surgery three years ago? 14.____
A(n)

I. osteoma
II. apical scar
III. radicular cyst
IV. dental granuloma
V. central giant cell granuloma
VI. denticle

The CORRECT answer is:

A. I, II, III, IV
B. I, IV
C. I, III
D. II, III, IV, V
E. II, III, V

15. Of the following, the one NOT an odontogenic lesion, histogenetically, is the 15.____

A. ameloblastoma
B. radicular cyst
C. complex odontoma
D. median palatal cyst
E. adenomatoid odontogenic tumor

16. Which of the following statements about syphilis is CORRECT? 16.____

A. The serological test for syphilis is strongly positive during the early primary stage.
B. The mucocutaneous lesions of secondary syphilis contain many spirochetes.
C. The typical lesion of secondary syphilis is called the gumma.

D. The chancre is not contagious.
E. All of the above

17. All of the following may have similar radiographic findings EXCEPT a(n) 17.____

A. ameloblastoma
B. radicular cyst
C. complex odontoma
D. eosinophilic granuloma
E. lateral periodontal cyst

18. Acute pulpitis, followed by localized degeneration of pulp tissue and the breakdown of leukocytes and bacteria, results in a lesion known as 18.____

A. a lateral periodontal abscess
B. acute hyperplastic pulpitis
C. a pulp abscess
D. a pulp stone
E. none of the above

19. All of the following diseases may be associated with pigmentation in oral regions EXCEPT 19.____

A. argyria
B. plumbism
C. Addison's disease
D. Albright's syndrome
E. Albers-Schönberg disease

20. A sclerotic zone in dentin is caused by 20.____

A. hypocalcification of odontoblastic processes and tubuli
B. mechanical, bacterial or chemical irritation
C. death of odontoblasts
D. tetracycline therapy
E. all of the above

21. The radiographic examination of a patient 20 years old disclosed a circumscribed radiolucent lesion 2 cm. in diameter in the mandibular right molar region. The lesion was sharply outlined but lacked a radiopaque periphery, was somewhat irregularly shaped, and extended 5 to 6 mm. above the apices of the molars and 10 mm. inferiorly toward the lower border of the mandible. There was no evidence of involvement of the cortex or expansion of the bone, and the lesion was asymptomatic. All teeth tested within a normal vitality range. 21.____
These findings would suggest

A. dentigerous cyst
B. radicular cyst
C. compound odontoma
D. hemorrhagic bone cyst
E. none of the above

22. The FIRST cell to arrive from the vascular bed to an injured area is the 22.____

A. eosinophil
B. lymphocyte
C. neutrophil
D. plasma cell
E. none of the above

23. The oral mucosal lesions of lichen planus, leukoplakia, and discoid lupus erythematosus have at least one common feature.
They are ALL 23.____

A. keratotic lesions
B. premalignant lesions
C. consequences of vitamin A deficiency
D. characterized by granulomatous proliferation
E. associated with local chronic irritation

24. Of the materials used in dentistry today, which are the MOST difficult to distinguish radiographically from caries? 24.____
I. Zinc oxide
II. Composite resin
III. Methyl methacrylate
IV. Zinc phosphate cement
V. Calcium hydroxide methyl cellulose paste
The CORRECT answer is:

A. I, II
B. I, III
C. II, IV
D. III, V
E. IV, V

25. The FIRST radiographic evidence of an acute dentoalveolar abscess is 25.____

A. extensive bone loss
B. rapid root resorption
C. thickening of the lamina dura
D. widening of the periodontal ligament space
E. none of the above

KEY (CORRECT ANSWERS)

1. E
2. D
3. C
4. D
5. A

6. C
7. D
8. C
9. C
10. B

11. B
12. C
13. A
14. D
15. D

16. B
17. C
18. C
19. E
20. B

21. D
22. C
23. A
24. D
25. D

TEST 2

DIRECTIONS: Each question or incomplete statement is followed by several suggested answers or completions. Select the one that BEST answers the question or completes the statement. *PRINT THE LETTER OF THE CORRECT ANSWER IN THE SPACE AT THE RIGHT.*

1. The pathologic basis for mongolism is 1.____

   A. excessive ingestion of fluorides
   B. trisomy 21
   C. disomy 21
   D. congenital syphilis
   E. nutritional deficiencies

2. In the chronic periapical granuloma, an important feature is the presence of epithelium. This epithelium may arise from 2.____
   I. the epithelial rests of Malassez
   II. respiratory epithelium of the maxillary sinus due to perforation of the sinus wall
   III. oral epithelium growing in a fistulous tract
   IV. oral epithelium proliferating from a periodontal pocket

   The CORRECT answer is:

   A. I *only*
   B. I, IV
   C. II, III
   D. I, III, IV
   E. All of the above

3. The tissue of origin of the MOST common malignancy of the palatal region is 3.____

   A. vascular tissue
   B. accessory salivary gland
   C. lymphatic tissue
   D. fibrous connective tissue
   E. stratified squamous epithelium

4. Dental plaque is composed PRIMARILY of water and 4.____
   I. bacteria
   II. extracellular matrix
   III. desquamative epithelial cells
   IV. food debris

   The CORRECT answer is:

   A. I, III
   B. II, III
   C. I, II
   D. III, IV
   E. All of the above

5. A craniopharyngioma is of interest to dentists because it histologically resembles the TYPICAL 5.____

   A. glioma
   B. hamartoma
   C. ameloblastoma
   D. squamous cell carcinoma
   E. none of the above

6. Characteristic histologic alterations found in squamous cell carcinoma would include: 6._____

   I. Large cells showing a distinct cell membrane
   II. Hyperchromatism
   III. Numerous mitotic figures some being abnormal
   IV. Epithelial pearls
   V. Nuclei varying little in size and shape

   The CORRECT answer is:

   A. I, II
   B. II, III, V
   C. II, III, IV, V
   D. I, III, V
   E. I, II, III, IV

7. A radicular cyst develops from 7._____

   A. ectopic salivary gland tissue in the jaws
   B. an epithelial odontogenic tumor such as ameloblastoma
   C. proliferation and extension of the epithelial attachment on the tooth
   D. proliferation of epithelial rests of Malassez in a periapical inflammatory lesion
   E. none of the above

8. In x-ray equipment, milliamperage controls the 8._____

   I. penetrating power of the radiation
   II. temperature of the cathode filament
   III. speed of the electrons
   IV. amount of radiation produced
   V. contrast

   The CORRECT answer is:

   A. I, III, V
   B. II, III, IV
   C. I, III
   D. II, IV
   E. III, V

9. Plummer-Vinson syndrome predisposes to carcinoma of the esophagus, oropharynx, and oral cavity. 9._____
   It is characterized by

   A. aplastic anemia
   B. normocytic hypochromic anemia
   C. microcytic hypochromic anemia
   D. macrocytic hyperchromic anemia
   E. Mediterranean anemia (Cooley's anemia)

10. Which of the following bone diseases are hereditary? 10._____

    I. Osteogenesis imperfecta
    II. Osteitis fibrosa cystica
    III. Cleidocranial dysostosis
    IV. Cherubism
    V. Multiple myeloma

    The CORRECT answer is:

    A. I, III, IV
    B. I, IV, V
    C. II, III, IV
    D. II, IV, V
    E. III, IV, V

11. During a routine dental examination, a radiolucency is observed at the apex of the mandibular right central incisor. The patient has no subjective symptoms, and the tooth pulp gives no response when tested with ice and with the vitalometer. The tooth is removed showing a firm mass attached to its apex. A histologic examination of the mass reveals fibrovascular connective tissue infiltrated with lymphocytes and plasma cells.
The microscopic findings in this case are MOST compatible with a diagnosis of 11.____

A. dental granuloma
B. chronic abscess
C. radicular cyst
D. apical scar

12. In certain bone diseases, localized or generalized radio-pacities may be noted radiographically reflecting an increase of bone mineralization or a decrease in bone resorption. 12.____
Which of the following diseases produce localized or generalized radiopacities?

I. Condensing osteitis
II. Cherubism
III. Albers-Schönberg disease
IV. Menopausal osteoporosis
V. Chronic sclerosing osteomyelitis

The CORRECT answer is:

A. I, II, III
B. I, III, V
C. I, IV, V
D. II, III, IV
E. II, IV, V

13. The characteristic oral manifestations of agranulocytosis (malignant neutropenia) consist of 13.____

A. acute stomatitis
B. gingival hyperplasia
C. multiple palatal petechine
D. ulceration of oral mucosa and gingiva
E. none of the above

14. Electrons lose their energy in the x-ray tube target PRIMARILY by 14.____

A. elastic scattering
B. production of x-ray
C. nuclear absorption
D. photoelectric and Compton effects
E. ionization and excitation

15. The intensity of x-radiation at any given distance from the source of radiation varies ______ the distance. 15.____

A. *inversely* with the square of
B. *directly* with the square of
C. *inversely* with
D. *directly* with
E. none of the above

16. Bremss strahlung refers to 16.____

A. radiation emitted upon breaking a nucleus
B. a process of nuclear de-excitation

C. electro-magnetic radiations from decelerated electrons
D. streams of electrons approaching the nucleus of a target atom
E. the mass to energy conversion

17. A two-year-old baby fractures his femur while crawling. He has pale blue sclera, porosity of the long bones, is extremely fragile, and is deaf. He suffers from 17.____

A. craniofacial dysostosis
B. osteogenesis imperfecta
C. cleidocranial dysostosis
D. Albers-Schönberg disease
E. mandibulofacial dysostosis

18. Three-phase generators are MORE efficient than single-phase generators in the production of x-rays because they 18.____

A. are less expensive to operate and install
B. have fewer parts
C. require more power to operate
D. provide near constant potential to the x-ray tube
E. none of the above

19. A periapical radiograph of a mandibular second premolar revealed a sharp right angle deviation of the apical one-third of the root. This is diagnostic of 19.____

A. dilaceration
B. concrescence
C. gemination
D. an odontoma
E. fusion

20. In any x-ray generator operated at low tube current, INCREASING the capacitance in the high-voltage circuit will 20.____

A. cause the average kilovoltage to increase
B. suppress inverse tube conduction
C. have no effect on system operation
D. decrease the x-ray output
E. increase the x-ray tube filament current

21. A one-year-old child who has bilateral facial swelling, fever, leukocytosis, and hyperostosis of the facial bones, with negative blood cultures, MOST likely has 21.____

A. Caffey-Smith syndrome
B. infectious parotitis
C. osteogenic sarcoma
D. osteomyelitis
E. cherubism

22. In the basic self-rectified x-ray machine circuit, if the x-ray tube was operating at 100 kVp, the peak potential difference between the primary and secondary of the filament transformer would be APPROXIMATELY ______ volts. 22.____

A. 50
B. 500
C. 5,000
D. 50,000
E. 100,000

23. The purpose of a step-up transformer in an x-ray machine is to INCREASE the 23.____

    A. milliamperage
    B. wavelength of the x-rays
    C. voltage to the tube filament
    D. potential between anode and cathode
    E. none of the above

24. The MAXIMUM energy of x-ray photons produced in an x-ray tube target depends upon the 24.____

    A. anode-cathode spacing
    B. peak kilovoltage
    C. x-ray tube current
    D. type of rectification
    E. transformer frequency

25. Changing the rectification of an x-ray machine from full-wave to half-wave while holding the kVp and filament current constant would 25.____

    A. *decrease* mA by a factor of 2
    B. *increase* mA by a factor of 2
    C. *have no effect on* mA
    D. *increase* the maximum tube loading by a factor of 2
    E. *decrease* the maximum tube loading by a factor of 2

KEY (CORRECT ANSWERS)

1.	B	11.	A
2.	E	12.	B
3.	B	13.	D
4.	C	14.	E
5.	C	15.	A
6.	E	16.	C
7.	D	17.	B
8.	D	18.	D
9.	C	19.	A
10.	A	20.	A

21. A
22. D
23. D
24. B
25. A

ORAL PATHOLOGY/RADIOGRAPHY

EXAMINATION SECTION
TEST 1

DIRECTIONS: Each question or incomplete statement is followed by several suggested answers or completions. Select the one that *BEST* answers the question or completes the statement. *PRINT THE LETTER OF THE CORRECT ANSWER IN THE SPACE AT THE RIGHT.*

1. *Three* inherent characteristics of radiographic film are: 1.____

   A. distortion, density, and contrast
   B. penumbra, contrast, and detail
   C. definition, contrast, and density
   D. definition, contrast, and distortion
   E. none of the above

2. Chronic osteomyelitis with proliferative periostitis of the mandible (Garré's chronic non-suppurative sclerosing osteitis) is characterized clinically *MAINLY* by marked 2.____

   A. endosteal bone formation
   B. periosteal bone formation
   C. resorption of cortical bone
   D. resorption of medullary bone
   E. none of the above

3. Hereditary hemorrhagic telangiectasia shows characteristic vascular lesions which occur *MOST* often on the 3.____

   A. lip
   B. tongue
   C. gingiva
   D. buccal mucosa
   E. salivary glands
   F. plica sublingualis

4. A 39-year-old woman has periodic burning of her buccal mucosa. Clinical examination reveals the presence of slightly elevated, grayish-white linear plaques. Biopsy of one of these reveals mild surface keratosis, acanthosis, vacuolation of many of the cells of the basal cell layer, and a dense inflammatory cellular infiltrate sharply delineated to the sub-epithelial connective tissue. 4.____
   The diagnosis *MOST* consistent with these changes is

   A. leukoedema
   B. leukoplakia
   C. lichen planus
   D. white-sponge nevus
   E. benign mucous membrane pemphigus

5. The *FIRST* consideration in the differential diagnosis of a painless palatal perforation would be 5.____

   A. syphilis
   B. histoplasmosis
   C. scrofuloderma
   D. actinomycosis
   E. none of the above

6. Of the following locations, the one in which the prognosis of epidermoid carcinoma is *LEAST* favorable is the 6.____

A. lower lip
B. upper lip
C. hard palate
D. buccalmucosa
E. posterior lateral border of the tongue

7. Which of the following conditions is *LEAST* likely to show oral manifestations? 7.____

A. Psoriasis
B. Pemphigoid
C. Periadenitis
D. Behcet's disease
E. Stevens-Johnson syndrome

8. Which of the following is *UNLIKELY* to cause enamel hypoplasia? 8.____

A. Rickets
B. Fluoride
C. Congenital syphilis
D. Exanthematous diseases
E. Cleidocranial dysostosis

9. Each of the following neuralgias is related to involvement of a specific nerve or ganglion. The nerve involved in each disease is listed after the disease. Which combination is *INCORRECT?* 9.____

A. Bell's palsy - 7th nerve
B. Herpes zoster - 5th nerve
C. Tic douloureaux - 5th nerve
D. Auriculotemporal syndrome - 5th nerve
E. Glossopharyngeal neuralgia - 9th nerve

10. Which of the following blood dyscrasias has a racial predilection? 10.____

A. Purpura
B. Leukemia
C. Hemophilia
D. Polycythemia
E. Sickle cell anemia

11. Intra-oral myoblastcmas occur *more* frequently in the 11.____

A. tongue
B. palate
C. gingivae
D. cheek along the line of occlusion of the teeth
E. None of the above

12. Epstein pearls are 12.____

A. the same as enamel pearls
B. imperfections in the tooth bud
C. seen in vitamin D deficiency
D. small keratin cysts of the newborn infant
E. none of the above

13. Serum hepatitis is caused by a(n) 13.____

A. virus
B. fungus
C. bacillus
D. allergic reaction to serum
E. reaction to local anesthetic

14. A 69-year-old man has an ulcerated lesion of the lower lip surrounded by a white plaque. The duration of the "sore" is approximately three weeks although, the "white patch" has been present for at least six months. The patient is a pipe smoker. Oral hygiene is poor and many teeth exhibit mobility.
Following the oral examination and case history, the procedure would be 14.____

A. plaque control
B. periodontal therapy
C. biopsy of the lesion on the lip
D. replacement of missing teeth with appropriate appliances
E. none of the above

15. A *constant* feature associated with the radicular cyst is a(n) 15.____

A. impacted tooth
B. missing tooth
C. nonvital tooth
D. anomalous tooth
E. compound odontoma

16. Lack of response at any level in a pulp vitality test can be used to *differentiate* between a 16.____

A. cementoma and a periapical granuloma
B. cementoma and an incisive canal cyst
C. globulomaxillary cyst and a traumatic bone cyst
D. periapical granuloma and an apical periodontal cyst
E. periapical granuloma and condensing osteitis

17. The *MOST* reliable *single* histologic criterion for a diagnosis of oral squamous cell carcinoma is 17.____

A. invasion
B. degeneration
C. pleomorphism
D. encapsulation
E. hyperchromatism

18. The *MOST* common complication of rheumatoid arthritis involving the temporamandibular joint is 18.____

A. subluxation
B. fibrous ankylosis
C. osteoma of the condyle
D. resorption of the condyle
E. synovial chondromatosis

19. In normal dental diagnostic procedures, the *PRINCIPAL* radiation hazard to the operator is produced by 19.____

A. gamma radiation
B. primary radiation
C. secondary radiation
D. all of the above
E. none of the above

20. Two or more teeth united only by cementum is designated as 20.____

A. fusion
B. sclerosis
C. gemination
D. dilaceration
E. concrescence

21. A maxillary lateral incisor with nonvital pulp and with periapical radiolucency is suitably treated and the root canal appropriately filled after two successive negative cultures of the apical areas.
The *MOST* common result of such treatment is 21.____

A. radiographic resolution of the periapical lesion within 2-3 weeks and an uneventful subsequent history
B. radiographic resolution of the periapical lesion within 6-12 months and an uneventful subsequent history
C. no change in the periapical area during 12 months or more, subsequent history otherwise uneventful
D. reappearance within 12 months of symptoms attributable to periapical infection

22. The characteristic lesion of herpes virus infections on the skin or mucous membranes is 22.____

A. necrosis
B. tumefaction
C. hyperkeratosis
D. abscess
E. vesicle

23. Which of the following have been considered as etiologic factors in the ankylosis of the temporomandibular joint? 23.____

I. Birth injury
II. Rheumatoid arthritis
III. Malunion of condylar fractures
IV. Abnormal intrauterine development
V. Trauma to the chin forcing the condyle against the glenoid fossa, particularly with bleeding into the joint space

The *CORRECT* answer is:

A. I, II, and III
B. I, III, and IV
C. I, IV, and V
D. II, III, and V
E. All of the above

24. Which of the following factors may *INCREASE* the size of the penumbra? 24.____

I. Small focal spot
II. Short object-film distance
III. Long source-object distance
IV. Movement of the tube

The *CORRECT* answer is:

A. I, II, and III
B. I and IV
C. II and IV
D. III and IV
E. IV *only*
F. All of the above

25. Of the materials used in dentistry today, which are the *MOST* difficult to distinguish radiographically from caries? 25.____

I. Zinc oxide
II. Composite resin
III. Methyl methacrylate
IV. Zinc phosphate cement
V. Calcium hydroxide methyl cellulose paste

The *CORRECT* answer is:

A. I and II
B. I and III
C. II and IV
D. III and V
E. IV and V

KEY (CORRECT ANSWERS)

1. C
2. B
3. A
4. C
5. A
6. E
7. A
8. E
9. D
10. E
11. A
12. D
13. A
14. C
15. C
16. A
17. A
18. B
19. C
20. E
21. B
22. E
23. E
24. E
25. D

TEST 2

DIRECTIONS: Each question or incomplete statement Is followed by several suggested answers or completions. Select the one that *BEST* answers the question or completes the statement. *PRINT THE LETTER OF THE CORRECT ANSWER IN THE SPACE AT THE RIGHT.*

1. Which of the following radiographic findings are characteristic of incisive canal cysts? 1.____
   I. A rounded delineated rarefaction
   II. No definite outline, with tendency to blend into the surrounding bone
   III. May be confused with a radicular cyst involving the anterior teeth
   IV. Located at the maxillary median line
   V. Located between canine and lateral incisor

   The *CORRECT* answer is:

   A. I and IV
   B. I, III, and IV
   C. I, III, and V
   D. II, III, and V
   E. II and IV

2. Which of the following bone diseases are hereditary? 2.____
   I. Osteogenesis imperfect a
   II. Osteitis fibrosa cystica
   III. Cleidocranial dysoscosis
   IV. Cherubism
   V. Multiple myeloma

   The *CORRECT* answer is:

   A. I, III, and IV
   B. I, IV, and V
   C. II, III, and IV
   D. II, IV, and V
   E. III, IV, and V

3. The effective focal spot is 3.____
   I. larger than the actual focal spot
   II. smaller than the actual focal spot
   III. in the shape of a square
   IV. in the shape of a rectangle

   The *CORRECT* answer is:

   A. I *only*
   B. I and III
   C. I and IV
   D. II and III
   E. II and IV

4. Apical root resorption is seen in 4.____
   I. fibrous dysplasia
   II. periapical cyst
   III. osteomalacia
   IV. periapical granuloma

   The *CORRECT* answer is:

   A. I *only*
   B. I, II, and III
   C. II and IV
   D. IV *only*
   E. All of the above

5. A firm, painless lesion of the palate had been present for at least 10 years and increased In size very slowly. The *MOST* likely diagnosis is 5.____

   A. torus palatinus
   B. retention cyst
   C. median palatal cyst
   D. pleomorphica denoma
   E. carcinoma of the ant rum

6. Histologic findings seen in a biopsy of an expansile poorly-demarcated, finely trabeculated radiopaque lesion in the maxilla of an 18-year-old girl consisted of randomly distributed spicules of osteoid scattered throughout a young connective tissue stroma. The *MOST* likely diagnosis is 6.____

   A. von Reeklinghausen's disease of bone
   B. fibrous dysplasia of bone
   C. Paget's disease of bone
   D. ameloblastoma
   E. osteosarcoma

7. Ground sections of early dental caries of enamel exhibit 7.____

   A. accentuated bands of Retzius and cross striations of enamel rods
   B. zones of fatty degeneration and sclerosis of enamel rods
   C. accentuated Owen's lines of contour and marked inter-globular areas
   D. zones of fatty degeneration and interglobular enamel,
   E. all of the above

8. A patient complains of numbness of the lower lip. There is no history of tooth extraction. The condition is *likely to* be related to 8.____

   A. infection
   B. metastatic neoplasm
   C. dental manipulation
   D. disease of the central nervous system
   E. none of the above

9. Characteristic dental findings of cleidocranial dysostosis include 9.____

   A. increased caries susceptibility
   B. enamel hypoplasia and lack of enamel formation
   C. juvenile periodontosis and subsequent premature loss of teeth
   D. failure of shedding and eruption, and numerous un-erupted supernumerary teeth
   E. all of the above

10. A young woman is admitted to the hospital. Petechiae on the oral mucous membrane and marginal gingival hemorrhage are noted. Platelet count is 45,000/mm.^{3} with increases in bleeding and clot retraction time. The RBC and differential are normal. *Probable* diagnosis is 10.____

    A. infectious mononucleosis
    B. thrombocytopenic purpura
    C. monocytic leukemia
    D. pernicious anemia
    E. hemophilia

11. A lesion was excised from the lower lip of a 14-year-old boy. It consisted of a central cavity filled with clear fluid and lined with granulation tissue only. Surface epithelium was extremely thin but intact. A few collections of salivary gland acini and bundles of skeletal muscle fibers were found deep to the lesion. The diagnosis is 11.____

    A. ranula
    B. fibroma
    C. mucocele
    D. sebaceous cyst
    E. pleomorphic adenoma

12. Leukemic gingivitis, because of spontaneous hemorrhage and necrosis, may be misdiagnosed as 12.____

A. necrotizing ulcerative gingivitis
B. thrombocytopenic purpura
C. infectious mononucleosis
D. desquamative gingivitis
E. none of the above

13. The sudden development of intensely red, wheat-like lesions on the oral mucosa which rapidly progress to thin-walled vesicles that rupture to leave superficial ulcerations covered by adherent yellowish-white membranes, suggests a diagnosis of 13.____

A. Behcet's disease
B. Reiter's syndrome
C. pemphigus vulgaris
D. erosive lichen planus
E. erythema multiforme

14. A patient exhibits multiple radiolucent areas in the jaw bones which simulate both peri-apical and perio-dontal lesions. The serum calcium is 13.5 mg% and serum phosphorus is 2.3 mg%. A biopsy from one of the radio-lucent areas reveals a giant cell lesion. The *MOST* likely diagnosis is 14.____

A. hyperparathyroidism
B. hypoparathyroidism
C. multiple myeloma
D. Hand-Schüller-Christian disease
E. myxedema

15. In inflammation of periodontal tissues, edema is *MOST* likely responsible for 15.____

A. alteration in contour of free gingiva
B. alteration in color of free gingiva
C. presence of pain
D. bone loss
E. blood loss

16. Absorption of photons produced by a 100-kVp x-ray machine operating at maximum output is *PRIMARILY* by 16.____

A. photoelectric effect *only*
B. compton effect *only*
C. 75% photoelectric, 25% compton
D. 50% photoelectric, 50% compton
E. photoelectric and compton effects in the ratio of 2 to 1

17. The *MOST* common malignancy within the oral cavity is the 17.____

A. ameloblastoma
B. adenocarcinoma
C. basal cell carcinoma
D. malignant mixed tumor
E. squamous cell carcinoma

18. An oral condition which predisposes an individual to an increase in incidence and rate of development of dental caries is 18.____

A. xerostomia
B. leukoplakia
C. pharyngitis
D. herpes stomatitis
E. median rhomboid glossitis

19. Cleft lip associated with cleft palate 19.____

A. results from the failure of the facial process to fuse
B. may cause an impediment of speech in children
C. may interfere with suckling in infants
D. can be easily treated by surgical closure
E. All of the above

20. Hyperplasia associated with the border of an ill-fitting denture (epulis fissuratum) is *MOST* similar histologically to 20.____

A. papilloma
B. verruca vulgaris
C. pyogenic granuloma
D. irritation fibroma
E. peripheral odontogenic fibroma with calcification

21. Radiographically, nutrient canals appear *only* 21.____

A. in the middle to lower G.I. tract
B. with the terminal point or area at the surface of bone
C. with the terminal point or area at the apices of teeth
D. as radiolucent areas
E. as radiopaque areas
F. None of the above

22. With a 20-film CMRS, a patient using a lead apron would be exposed to approximately 22.____

	Facial Exposure	Gonad Exposure
A.	2-3 R	0.5 R
B.	3-4 R	0.5 R
C.	3-5 R	0.5 mR
D.	3-5 R	0.03 mR
E.	5-7 R	0.005 mR
F.	7-9 R	0.003 mR

23. Some microorganisms produce a diffuse, spreading inflammatory reaction due to the elaboration of 23.____

A. coagulase
B. peroxidase
C. bradykinin
D. leukotaxine
E. hyaluronidase

24. An 18-year-old man complains of a painful swelling in the palate. Examination reveals a soft, fluctuant, tender mass in the midline of the hard palate. The teeth test vital and there is no evidence of periodontal disease. Radiographs, however, reveal a well-defined radiolucency between the roots of the maxillary central incisors. Clinical and radiographic findings are *compatible* with the diagnosis of a 24.____

A. lateral periodontal cyst
B. globulomaxillary cyst
C. incisive canal cyst
D. nasolabial cyst
E. All of the above

25. "Sulfur granules" are of diagnostic value in suspected cases of 25.____

A. histoplasmosis
B. actinomycosis
C. lead sulfide tissue deposits
D. scrofula
E. furunculosis

KEY (CORRECT ANSWERS)

1. B
2. A
3. C
4. C
5. D
6. B
7. A
8. B
9. D
10. B
11. C
12. A
13. E
14. A
15. A
16. D
17. E
18. A
19. E
20. D
21. D
22. D
23. E
24. C
25. B

ORAL PATHOLOGY/RADIOGRAPHY EXAMINATION SECTION TEST 1

DIRECTIONS: Each question or incomplete statement is followed by several suggested answers or completions. Select the one that *BEST* answers the question or completes the statement. *PRINT THE LETTER OF THE CORRECT ANSWER IN THE SPACE AT THE RIGHT.*

1. An excisional biopsy of a 5 mm. nodule on the side of the tongue was diagnosed histologically as fibroma. 1.____
This patient should have

   A. radiation therapy to the site of biopsy
   B. re-excision with wider margins
   C. hemisection of the tongue
   D. no additional therapy
   E. complete rest and relaxation

2. The etiology of multiple neurofibromatosis is 2.____

   A. a virus
   B. an injury
   C. genetic
   D. endocrine dysfunction
   E. none of the above

3. If a caries-susceptible animal is born and raised in a germ-free environment, it will develop carious lesions in its teeth if 3.____

   A. it eats either a low carbohydrate or a high carbohydrate diet
   B. specific strains of cariogenic microorganisms are introduced
   C. it eats a high carbohydrate diet
   D. other germ-free animals are kept in the same chamber
   E. None of the above

4. The process of dental caries consists of a 4.____

   A. dissolution of the enamel matrix by proteolytic bacteria and a destruction of dentin by acidogenic microorganisms
   B. demineralization of tooth substance and lysis of organic elements by an adherent community of microorganisms
   C. dissolution of enamel and dentin by acids produced by the bacterial microcosm
   D. dissolution of the tooth by acids exclusively
   E. None of the above

5. The *MOST* common cyst in the oral regions is a(n) 5.____

   A. median cyst
   B. radicular cyst
   C. follicular cyst
   D. nasolabial cyst
   E. epidermal inclusion cyst

6. An area of radiolucency about the crown of an unerupted tooth which has obviously completed its development suggests a(n) 6.____

   A. median cyst
   B. impact ion
   C. dentingerous cyst
   D. primordial cyst
   E. None of the above

7. Chronic hyperplastic pulpitis is *essentially* a 7.____

   A. necrotizing lesion
   B. suppurative lesion
   C. proliferation of chronically inflamed pulp tissue
   D. very sensitive, painful lesion
   E. All of the above

8. The acute periapical abscess 8.____

   A. may be accompanied by regional lymphadenopathy
   B. is usually asymptomatic
   C. has inevitable severe systemic manifestations
   D. is not relieved by drainage
   E. None of the above

9. *MOST* cases of pulpitis are caused by 9.____

   A. injudicious cavity preparation
   B. excessive heat incident to dry polishing of restoration
   C. chemical irritation from sterilizing agents or filling materials
   D. bacterial invasion from a carious lesion
   E. bacterial invasion from the bloodstream
   F. severe trauma

10. A periapical radiograph of the mandibular premolar region reveals a completely embedded supernumerary tooth, superimposed on the roots of both premolars. With another film in the same position, a second projection is made from a more mesial horizontal angulation. In the second film, the image of the supernumerary tooth appears to have shifted distally from its original position. 10.____
    This would indicate that the supernumerary tooth lies

    A. buccal to the premolars
    B. lingual to the premolars
    C. in the same plane as the premolars
    D. All of the above
    E. None of the above

11. An inflamed capillary hemangioma of the oral cavity looks similar, microscopically, to a(n) 11.____

    A. nevus
    B. neurofibroma
    C. angiosarcoma
    D. pyogenic granuloma
    E. None of the above

12. Caries on a proximal surface usually *starts* 12.____

    A. buccal to the contact zone and the marginal ridge
    B. lingual to the contact zone and the marginal ridge
    C. between the contact zone and the dentinoenamel junction

D. between the contact zone and the crest of the gingiva
E. distal to the contact zone at the contact zone

13. The radiographic examination of a patient 20 years old disclosed a circumscribed radiolucent lesion 2 cm. in diameter in the mandibular right molar region. The lesion was sharply outlined but lacked a radiopaque periphery, was somewhat irregularly shaped, and extended 5 to 6 mm. above the apices of the molars and 10 mm. inferiorly toward the lower border of the mandible. There was no evidence of involvement of the cortex or expansion of the bone and the lesion was asymptomatic. All teeth tested within a normal vitality range. 13.____
These findings would suggest

A. dentigerous cyst
B. radicular cyst
C. compound odontoma
D. simple bone cyst
E. none of the above

14. The efficiency of x-ray production in an x-ray machine depends upon the 14.____
I. target material
II. applied kilovoltage
III. output of the machine
IV. cooling curve of the machine
The *CORRECT* answer is:

A. I, II, and IV
B. I and II
C. II and III
D. III *only*
E. III and IV

15. A patient exhibits marked attrition of the deciduous and permanent teeth and radiographs reveal a marked tendency toward obliteration of many pulp canals. The patient's mother and brother also have had histories of this condition. 15.____
The *MOST* likely diagnosis is

A. enamel hypoplasla
B. enamel hypomaturation
C. dentinogenesis Imperfecta
D. mottled enamel
E. none of the above

16. The *PRIMARY* cause of radiation damage is 16.____

A. ionization
B. direct effect
C. genetic damage
D. indirect effect
E. none of the above

17. A patient has a swelling of long standing at the ala of the nose on the left side. Examination reveals a swelling in the floor of the nostril and beneath the upper lip. There is no pain and regional teeth are vital. Radiographs show no bone change. 17.____
The *preliminary* diagnosis would be

A. alveolar abscess
B. incisive canal cyst
C. nasolabial cyst
D. dermoid cyst
E. maxillary sinusitis

18. Microscopically, the *PRIMARY* cells which characterize eosinophilic granuloma are 18.____

A. fibroblasts
B. histocytes
C. plasma cells
D. epithelial cells
E. eosinophils

19. The rarefaction occurring in the bone from an infected deciduous molar, as studied radiographically, *MOST* frequently appears 19.____

A. about the apices
B. between two teeth
C. in the bifurcation
D. around the developing permanent tooth
E. as a uniform widening of the periodontal ligament space

20. Multiple giant cell lesions of bone are associated with 20.____

A. pituitary deficiency
B. hyperparathyroidism
C. Addison's disease
D. hypothyroidism
E. diabetes

21. The giant cell granuloma is characterized by all of the following histopathologic features *EXCEPT* 21.____

A. foci of hemorrhage
B. scattered eosinophils
C. deposits of hemosiderin
D. many multinucleated giant cells
E. a stroma consisting of fusiform and round fibroblasts

22. All of the following diseases may be associated with pigmentation in oral regions *EXCEPT* 22.____

A. argyria
B. plumbism
C. Addison's disease
D. Albright's syndrome
E. Peutz-Jeghers syndrome
F. Albers-Schonberg disease

23. A number of conditions may present as periapical radio-lucencies. These include all of the following *EXCEPT* 23.____

A. dental granuloma
B. periapical cemental dysoplasia
C. met astatic car cinema of the breast
D. multiple myeloma
E. hypercementosis

24. Congenital syphilis and Hutchanson's triad include each of the following *EXCEPT* 24.____

A. Ghon complex
B. mulberry molars
C. notched incisors
D. interstitial keratitis
E. nerve deafness, rhagades, saddle nose

25. All of the following may have similar radiographic findings *EXCEPT* a(n) 25.____

A. ameloblastoma
B. radicular cyst
C. complex odontoma
D. eosinophilic granuloma
E. lateral periodontal cyst

KEY (CORRECT ANSWERS)

1. D
2. C
3. B
4. B
5. B

6. C
7. C
8. A
9. D
10. A

11. D
12. D
13. D
14. A
15. C

16. A
17. C
18. B
19. C
20. B

21. B
22. F
23. E
24. A
25. C

TEST 2

DIRECTIONS: Each question or Incomplete statement is followed by several suggested answers or completions. Select the one that *BEST* answers the question or completes the statement. *PRINT THE LETTER OF THE CORRECT ANSWER IN THE SPACE AT THE RIGHT.*

1. *Which* of the following groups of conditions has lesions of the oral mucosa which may pass through a stage in which they appear as vesicles? 1.____

   A. Herpes simplex, pemphigus, and varicella
   B. Verruca vulgaris, herpes simplex, and tuberculous ulcer
   C. Hyperkeratosis, mucous patches, and Fordyce granules
   D. Pemphigus, erythema multiforme, and angionerotic edema
   E. Koplik spots, purpura hemorrhagica, and cancrum oris

2. *Which* of the following regions in the crown of a tooth is often mistaken for caries in the dental film? 2.____

   A. Pulp horn
   B. Marginal ridge
   C. Secondary dentin
   D. Cementoenamel junction
   E. None of the above

3. A radiograph reveals a radiolucent shadow at the apex: of the maxillary right central incisor. There is no break in the continuity of the lamina dura, and the tooth responds normally to the pulp tester. There are no clinical signs or symptoms. 3.____
   What is the *MOST* probable explanation of the radiolucent shadow?

   A. Trauma
   B. Infection
   C. Chemical artifact
   D. Anatomic landmark
   E. None of the above

4. *Which* of the following clinical manifestations of syphilis may involve oral mucous membranes? 4.____

   I. Mucous patch
   II. Chancre
   III. Gumma
   IV. Tabes dorsalis
   V. Hepar lobatum

   The *CORRECT* answer is:

   A. I *only*
   B. I, II, and IV
   C. I and III
   D. I, II, and III
   E. II, III, IV, and V
   F. All of the above

5. There is a radiopaque area on the distal root of the mandibular right first molar. The radiographic diagnosis would probably be 5.____

   A. osteoma
   B. cementoma
   C. eburnated bone
   D. condensing osteitis
   E. none of the above

6. The radiopacity that frequently obliterates the apices of maxillary molars when using the bisecting principle of intra-oral radiography is the 6.____

   A. zygoma and the zygomatic process of the maxilla
   B. orbital process of the zygomatic bone
   C. palatine bone and the zygoma

D. maxillary sinus
E. None of the above

7. *Which* of the following lesions is the *MOST* frequent cause of resorption at the root apex? 7.____

A. Cementoma
B. Fibrous dysplasia
C. Primordial cyst
D. Periapical granuloma
E. Globulomaxillary cyst

8. *Which* of the following has been determined to be the *MOST* cariogenic carbohydrate? 8.____

A. Starch
B. Sucrose
C. Glucose
D. Glycogen
E. Dextranase
F. All are sugars and, thus, equally cariogenic

9. A 43-year-old man has a buccal lesion characterized by deep ulceration. The lesion has a red, raised border and is 0.5 cm. in diameter. The patient indicates that the lesion is painful, that it has been present for about four weeks, and that he has suffered from such lesions as long as he can remember, as evidenced by numerous scarred are as. 9.____
Which of the following conditions is *MOST* suspect on the basis of the clinical findings and the case history?

A. Pemphigus
B. Herpes simplex
C. Erythema multiforme
D. Periadenitis mucosa necrotica recurrens
E. All of the above

10. A patient has a 7x5 cm. soft swelling at the angle of the mandible anterior to the sternomastoid muscle. The patient states that he has been aware of the swelling most of his life and that there has never been any pain associated with the swelling. The regional lymph nodes are nonpalpable. Blood and urine tests are within normal limits. Radiographic surveys of the teeth, jaws, and cervical spine are negative. Aspiration of the swelling reveals a yellow-brown fluid. 10.____
What condition is *MOST* suggestive on the basis of the clinical examination and the laboratory findings?

A. Submylohyoid dermoid cyst
B. Follicular ameloblastoma
C. Thyroglossal duct cyst
D. Branchial cleft cyst
E. None of the above

11. Using "B" speed film exposure to the patient at 3 feet is 1 roentgen. *What* would the exposure be with "D" speed film at 6 feet? (Assume all other exposure factors to be the same.) 11.____

A. 1/8 R
B. 1/4 R
C. 1/2 R
D. 3/4 R
E. 7/8 R

12. Of the following salivary gland lesions, *which* is usually associated with the sicca syndrome? 12.____

A. Mixed tumor
B. Adenoid cystic carcinoma
C. Mucoepidermoid carcinoma

D. Benign lymphoepithelial lesion
E. None of the above

13. *Which* of the following would *MOST* likely be associated with a nonvital tooth? 13.____

A. Radicular cyst
B. Internal resorption
C. Periapical cementoma
D. Hyperplastic pulpitis
E. Active formation of a true denticle

14. An oral examination of a three-year-old child revealed only deciduous canines and first molars present. During general observation of this child, it was noted that the complexion was very light, the hair was fine and light, and the overall appearance of the face was that of an older person. 14.____
Which of the following conditions is suggested?

A. Cleidocranial dysostosis
B. Osteogenesis imperfecta
C. Hereditary ectodermal dysplasia
D. Crouzon's disease
E. All of the above

15. A patient is concerned about yellow spots in his mouth. Examination reveals many chamois colored, flat or slightly elevated spots distributed bilaterally on the buccal mucosa. There are no other clinical findings. 15.____
What condition is *MOST* suspect?

A. Chickenpox
B. Lichen planus
C. Fordyce spots
D. Koplik spots
E. Herpangina

16. A congenital epulis of the newborn is *MOST* likely to resemble microscopically a(n) 16.____

A. epithelial pearl
B. gingivitis granuloma gravidarium
C. aberrant sebaceous gland
D. granular cell myoblastoma
E. peripheral giant cell granuloma

17. In radiography, the periapical area refers to the 17.____

A. dental pulp
B. gingival area
C. investing tissue
D. root tip area
E. apical foramen

18. In radiography, the dental assistant should 18.____

A. always hold the film in the patient's mouth
B. hold the film when requested by the patient
C. in each case ask the dentist whether the film is to be held
D. not hold the film in the patient's mouth
E. do none of the above

19. The part of the x-ray machine which automatically controls the length of time for an exposure is called a(n) 19.____

A. volt-meter
B. time switch
C. milliammeter
D. safety valve
E. ammeter

20. The substance *MOST* commonly used for protection against x-ray radiation is 20.____

A. zinc
B. steel
C. lead
D. porcelain
E. platinum

21. The developer for x-ray reproductions should always be kept at a temperature of approximately ______ degrees F 21.____

A. 55-65
B. 65-75
C. 75-85
D. 85-95
E. 95-105

22. The terms "visual method" and "time temperature method" refer to 22.____

A. x-ray film development
B. the administration of an anesthesia
C. oral surgery
D. sterilization procedures
E. all of the above

23. Roentgenology is *CHIEFLY* concerned with the study of 23.____

A. dental diseases
B. x-ray films
C. mechanical disorders of the mouth
D. operative dentistry
E. residual effects of contamination

24. Which of the following protective procedures for operator is (are) correct? 24.____
Operator. For his protection, the person taking radiographs must;

I. Wear his monitoring device as prescribed
II. Have the patient or another person not habitually exposed to radiation hold the film during exposure
III. Refrain from holding the tube housing during exposure
IV. Stand inside the safety of the protective screen or booth during exposure.

The *CORRECT* answer is:

A. I only
B. I, II
C. I, II, III
D. I, II, III, IV
E. None of the above

25. Which of the following protective procedures for patient is (are) correct? 25.____
Patient. To protect the patient, the operator should:

I. Check the patient's medical history
II. Take no radiographs which have not been requested by a dental officer
III. Use care in exposing, processing, recording, and mfiling radiographic film so as to minimize the need for "retakes"
IV. Use that voltage, type of film (high-speed), and technique of exposure which will produce the desired diagnostic result in the finished radiograph with minimal radiation exposure
V. Use a lead apron when it is indicated

The *CORRECT* answer is:

A. I *only*
B. I, II
C. I, II, III
D. I, II, III, IV
E. I, II, III, IV, V

KEY (CORRECT ANSWERS)

1. A
2. D
3. D
4. D
5. D
6. A
7. D
8. B
9. D
10. D
11. A
12. D
13. A
14. C
15. C
16. D
17. D
18. D
19. B
20. C
21. B
22. A
23. B
24. D
25. E

ORAL PATHOLOGY / RADIOGRAPHY

EXAMINATION SECTION
TEST 1

DIRECTIONS: Each question or incomplete statement is followed by several suggested answers or completions. Select the one that BEST answers the question or completes the statement. *PRINT THE LETTER OF THE CORRECT ANSWER IN THE SPACE AT THE RIGHT.*

Questions 1-5.

DIRECTIONS: Questions 1 through 5 are to be answered on the basis of the following illustration.

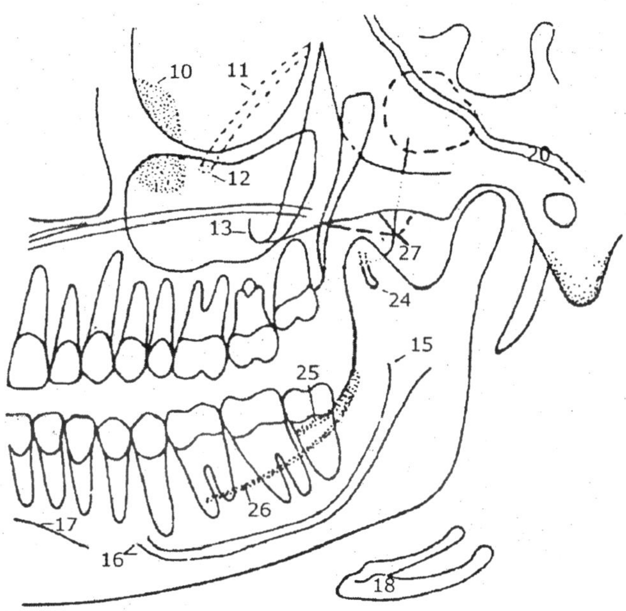

1. The structure labeled 10 is the 1.____

   A. mastoid
   B. sphenoidal sinus
   C. ethmoid sinus
   D. anterior nasal spine
   E. pterygomaxillary fissure

2. The structure labeled 12 is the 2.____

   A. nasal fossa
   B. ethmoid sinus
   C. maxillary sinus
   D. infratemporal crest
   E. infraorbital foramen

3. The structure labeled 16 is the 3.____

A. genial tubercle
B. mental foramen
C. mandibular foramen
D. internal oblique line
E. external oblique line

4. The structure labeled 17 is the 4.____

A. hyoid bone
B. hard palate
C. mental process
D. malar process
E. incisive foramen

5. The structure labeled 24 is the 5.____

A. sella turcica
B. hamular process
C. zygomatic arch
D. lateral pterygoid plate
E. external auditory meatus

6. A man who suffered a displaced mandibular fracture some time ago complains of pain. The pain is in the old fracture site, near the mental foramen. Palpation reveals a freely movable, exquisitely tender mass in the described area. 6.____
The BEST preoperative diagnosis is

A. neurilemoma
B. neurofibroma
C. traumatic neuroma
D. von Recklinghausen disease
E. none of the above

7. A 0.7 cm. pedunculated, white, rough-surfaced growth occurring on the hard palate is MOST likely a(n) 7.____

A. adenoid cystic carcinoma
B. pleomorphic adenoma
C. keratoacanthoma
D. papilloma
E. fibroma

8. Selection of the proper kilovoltage for dental films is influenced by 8.____

A. type of timer
B. target-film distance
C. temperature of the developing solution
D. diameter of the primary beam of radiation
E. density of the tissues to be radiographed

9. Acantholysis is an IMPORTANT diagnostic feature in 9.____

A. pemphigus
B. lichen planus
C. erythema multiforme
D. lupus erythematosus
E. none of the above

10. A healthy pulp recovers from minimal injury by 10.____

A. anachoresis
B. degeneration
C. deposition of dentin

D. formation of a polyp
E. formation of granulation tissue

11. A dens in dente is USUALLY caused by a(n) 11.____

A. abnormal proliferation of pulp tissue
B. denticle formation within the pulp tissue
C. deep invagination of the enamel organ during formation
D. supernumerary tooth bud enclaved within a normal tooth
E. normal tooth bud enclaved within another during tooth formation

12. In the healing of an ulcer, the epithelium that eventually will cover the defect is derived from 12.____

A. intact epithelium at the ulcer margin
B. metaplasia of fibroblasts to epithelial cells
C. transformation of fibrinous exudate to epithelium
D. transformation of endothelial cells to epithelial cells
E. none of the above

13. A progressive INCREASE in mandibular length and in mandibular interdental spacing in an adult patient is characteristic of 13.____

A. periodontosis
B. hypothyroidism
C. hyperpituitarism
D. hypoadrenalism
E. hyperparathyroidism

14. The PRINCIPAL reason for placing an aluminum filter in the primary beam of radiation is to 14.____

A. reduce exposure time
B. decrease development time of the films
C. reduce radiation to the skin of the patient
D. obtain greater definition of the images of teeth
E. increase exposure time

15. A friable, elevated, bright purplish-red tumorlike mass with a raspberry appearance, located MOST frequently on the gingiva and consisting of granulation tissue with young fibroblasts, proliferating capillaries, and inflammatory cells is 15.____

A. a fibroma
B. a pyogenic granuloma
C. Dilantin® hyperplasia
D. a peripheral giant cell granuloma
E. a radicular cyst

16. The exact mechanism of carbohydrate degradation to form acids in the oral cavity by bacterial action is not known. However, present thinking suggests that 16.____

A. dental plaque is the only responsible factor
B. dextran synthesis is the ultimate causative factor
C. it most likely occurs through enzymatic breakdown of sugar

D. amino acids are the factors responsible for carbohydrate degradation and bacterial action
E. none of the above

17. The oral lesion of syphilis that is HIGHLY infective is a 17.____

A. gumma
B. Koplik spot
C. mucous patch
D. tabes dorsal is
E. Hutchinson incisor

18. Symptoms of pain and tenderness upon palpation of the temporomandibular joint are USUALLY associated with 18.____

A. impacted mandibular third molars
B. flaccid paralysis of the painful side of the face
C. flaccid paralysis of the nonpainful side of the face
D. excitability of the second division of the fifth nerve
E. deviation of the jaw to the painful side upon opening the mouth

19. Examination discloses a slightly elevated, somewhat mamillated, nonulcerated, non-tender, firm, reddish area measuring approximately 1.0 x 1.5 cm. on the dorsal surface of the tongue just anterior to the circumvallate papillae. The patient was not aware of the lesion. The remainder of the examination is within normal limits. This lesion MOST probably represents 19.____

A. a cyst of the glands of Blandin and Nuhn
B. median rhomboid glossitis
C. squamous cell carcinoma
D. migratory glossitis
E. none of the above

20. The USUAL radiographic appearance of an osteogenic sarcoma is described as a 20.____

A. sunburst pattern with radiopaque strands extending from the cortical plates
B. cotton-wool appearance with an irregular peripheral border
C. multicystic radiolucency with a soap-bubble appearance
D. discrete radiolucency with regular borders
E. none of the above

21. An exposure of 2 roentgens is recorded at a point 8 inches from the target of an x-ray machine. 21.____
In the same beam, the exposure at 4 inches would be _______ R.

A. 4 B. 6 C. 8 D. 12 E. 16

22. In erythema multiforme, TYPICAL oral involvement consists of 22.____

A. fissured tongue
B. acute gingivitis
C. diffuse mucosal ulcerations
D. vesicles on the soft palate
E. white striations on the buccal mucosa

23. An INCREASED incidence of neurogenic sarcoma might be expected in patients with a previous diagnosis of 23.____

A. schwannoma
B. neurilemoma
C. acoustic neuroma
D. neurofibromatosis
E. amputation (traumatic) neuroma

24. A 41-year-old woman has periodic burning of her buccal mucosa. Clinical examination reveals the presence of slightly elevated grayish-white linear plaques. Biopsy of one of these reveals mild surface keratosis, acanthosis, vacuolation of many of the cells of the basal cell layer, and a dense inflammatory cellular infiltrate sharply delineated to the sub-epithelial connective tissue. The diagnosis MOST consistent with these changes is 24.____

A. leukoedema
B. lichen planus
C. white sponge nevus
D. epithelial dysplasia
E. mucous membrane pemphigoid

25. In a pulp, lack of response to vitality tests can be used to differentiate between a 25.____

A. cementoma and a periapical granuloma
B. cementoma and an incisive canal cyst
C. periapical granuloma and a periapical cyst
D. periapical granuloma and condensing osteitis
E. globulomaxillary cyst and a traumatic bone cyst

KEY (CORRECT ANSWERS)

1. C
2. E
3. B
4. C
5. B
6. C
7. D
8. E
9. A
10. C
11. C
12. A
13. C
14. C
15. B
16. C
17. C
18. E
19. B
20. A
21. C
22. C
23. D
24. B
25. A

TEST 2

DIRECTIONS: Each question or incomplete statement is followed by several suggested answers or completions. Select the one that BEST answers the question or completes the statement. *PRINT THE LETTER OF THE CORRECT ANSWER IN THE SPACE AT THE RIGHT.*

1. Mucoceles MOST commonly arise as a result of 1.____

   A. rupture of a salivary duct
   B. partial or complete compression of the salivary acini
   C. inflammatory changes in the glandular interstitial tissue
   D. partial or complete obstruction of the salivary duct by calculus
   E. any of the above

2. A patient presents with a 3 cm. ulceration of three months' duration on the lateral border of the tongue. The lesion is fixed, indurated and painless. There is an associated lymphadenopathy on the same side. Treatment of choice should include 2.____

   A. a cytologic smear
   B. an incisional biopsy
   C. an excisional biopsy
   D. antibiotic therapy
   E. none of the above

3. A high titer of serum heterophile antibodies is found in patients with 3.____

   A. herpangina
   B. hepatitis A
   C. actinomycosis
   D. herpes simplex
   E. infectious mononucleosis

4. A patient has high serum calcium, high alkaline phosphatase, and low serum phosphorus levels. Intraoral radiographs reveal marked generalized radiolucency of bone. The MOST probable diagnosis is 4.____

   A. hyperostosis
   B. osteitis deformans
   C. hypoparathyroidism
   D. none of the above
   E. any of the above

5. Severe pain that arises following sectioning or injury to a peripheral nerve and that may occur following tooth extraction is characteristic of 5.____

   A. causalgia
   B. Horner syndrome
   C. Meniere disease
   D. myasthenia gravis
   E. auriculotemporal syndrome

6. A dental finding FREQUENTLY observed in cases of Paget disease of bone is 6.____

   A. hypercementosis
   B. apical root resorption
   C. internal resorption of the pulp
   D. widening of the periodontal ligament space
   E. none of the above

7. Of the following conditions, gingival involvement would be UNUSUAL in 7.____

A. pemphigoid
B. primary herpes
C. recurrent aphthae
D. pyogenic granuloma
E. all of the above

8. A 21-year-old female presents with complete absence of clavicles, a narrow arched palate, and prolonged retention of primary teeth. 8.____
The MOST probable diagnosis is

A. osteopetrosis
B. achondroplasia
C. Marfan syndrome
D. Pierre Robin syndrome
E. cleidocranial dysostosis

9. A 30-year-old patient presents with an asymptomatic, doughy, soft, 2 cm. swelling of the lateral neck which has been present for months. The swelling recently enlarged as a result of an upper respiratory infection. The MOST likely diagnosis is 9.____

A. scrofula
B. Hodgkin disease
C. cat scratch fever
D. cervicofacial actinomycosis
E. cervical lymphoepithelial cyst

10. Bohn nodules or Epstein pearls are cysts that arise from 10.____

A. squamous epithelium of the mucosa
B. connective tissue of the mucosa
C. rests of Malassez
D. dental lamina
E. none of the above

11. Monostotic fibrous sysplasia is MOST similar histologically to 11.____

A. ossifying fibroma
B. giant cell granuloma
C. aneurysmal bone cyst
D. Paget disease of bone
E. none of the above

12. Giant cell granuloma is MOST often associated with 12.____

A. hypoparathyroidism
B. hyperparathyroidism
C. hypothyroidism
D. hyperthyroidism
E. none of the above

13. The odontogenic tumor FREQUENTLY found in children and associated with an unerupted tooth in the anterior portion of the jaws is 13.____

A. odontogenic myxoma
B. ameloblastic fibroma
C. cementifying fibroma
D. odontogenic adenomatoid tumor
E. calcifying epithelial odontogenic tumor

14. In radiography, a longer gray scale of contrast can be achieved by 14.____

A. *decreasing* the filtration
B. *increasing* the kilovoltage

C. *increasing* the milliamperage
D. *decreasing* the milliampere seconds
E. *increasing* the focal spot-skin distance

15. Nicotine stomatitis is characterized by 15.____

A. ulceration of the tonsillar crypt
B. inflamed orifice of the Stenson duct
C. local exfoliation of the filiform papillae
D. ulceration of the inner surface of the lip
E. inflamed orifices of the palatal mucous glands

16. A 65-year-old man presents with a 0.8 cm. elevated, crusted lesion on the side of the nose. The patient states that the lesion has been present for several months, and it never quite heals. 16.____
The MOST likely clinical diagnosis is

A. basal cell carcinoma
B. lupus erythematosus
C. verucca vulgaris
D. sebaceous cyst
E. psoriasis

17. The MOST common primary malignant tumor of bone in patients under 25 years of age is 17.____

A. liposarcoma
B. chondrosarcoma
C. multiple myeloma
D. osteogenic sarcoma
E. reticulum cell sarcoma

18. An acute infectious inflammatory condition characterized by punched-out ulcers of marginal and papillary gingivae with symptoms of salivation, metallic taste, and pain is 18.____

A. agranulocytosis
B. erythema multiforme
C. streptococcal stomatitis
D. acute herpetic stomatitis
E. acute ulcerative gingivostomatitis

19. Radiographically, a benign neoplasm in bone may be differentiated from a malignant one because in the benign lesion 19.____
I. margins are irregular and fade imperceptibly into surrounding bone
II. the cortex tends to remain intact but may be thinned and the part involved expanded
III. margins are usually defined and demarcated from surrounding bone
IV. there may often be a perforation of the periosteum
The CORRECT answer is:

A. I, II
B. I, II, IV
C. II, III
D. II, III, IV
E. III, IV

20. The light image of a single hair appears on a radiograph which was exposed in a cassette. 20.____
To produce this image, the hair must have been located
   I. on the front of the cassette
   II. between the film and the front intensifying screen
   III. between the film and the rear intensifying screen
   IV. on the film during development
   V. on the film during fixing
The CORRECT answer is:

A. I, II, III
B. I, III, V
C. I, IV, V
D. II, III, IV
E. III, IV, V

21. Characteristic features of proximal caries on premolars and molars are that they spread 21.____
   I. cone-shaped into the enamel, the base of the cone being the deepest part
   cone-shaped into the enamel, the apex of the cone being the deepest part
   II. in the dentin in a conical form, the apex pointing toward the pulp
   III. in the dentin in a conical form, the base pointing toward the pulp
The CORRECT answer is:

A. I, III
B. I, IV
C. II, III
D. II, IV
E. II *only*

22. Clinical features of Sjögren syndrome include 22.____
   I. xerostomia
   II. rheumatoid arthritis
   III. keratoconunctivitis sicca
The CORRECT answer is:

A. I, II
B. I, III
C. II, III
D. III *only*
E. All of the above

23. Oral mucosal pigmentation is characteristic of 23.____
   I. Papillon-Lefèvre syndrome
   II. Addison disease
   III. Mikulicz disease
   IV. Peutz-Jeghers syndrome
The CORRECT answer is:

A. I, II, III
B. I, III
C. II, IV
D. IV *only*
E. All of the above

24. Which of the following characterize the dental pulp in old age? 24.____
   I. Increased fibrosis
   II. Decreased cellularity
   III. Decreased vascularity
   IV. Increased calcification
The CORRECT answer is:

A. I, II
B. I, II, IV
C. I, III, IV
D. III, IV
E. All of the above

25. Sialoliths are MOST commonly found during radiographic examination of the 25.____

A. parotid duct
B. maxillary sinus
C. submandibular duct
D. sublingual gland duct
E. minor salivary glands

KEY (CORRECT ANSWERS)

1. A
2. B
3. E
4. D
5. A
6. A
7. C
8. E
9. E
10. D
11. A
12. B
13. D
14. B
15. E
16. A
17. D
18. E
19. C
20. D
21. C
22. E
23. C
24. E
25. C

TEST 3

DIRECTIONS: Each question or incomplete statement is followed by several suggested answers or completions. Select the one that BEST answers the question or completes the statement. *PRINT THE LETTER OF THE CORRECT ANSWER IN THE SPACE AT THE RIGHT.*

1. Which of the following is ESSENTIAL to the development of caries? 1._____

   A. High carbohydrate diet
   B. Genetic predisposition to the disease
   C. Presence of bacterial plaque on the tooth
   D. Increased numbers of bacteria in saliva
   E. Total absence or decreased levels of salivary immunoglobulin A (IgA)

2. Which of the following has been determined to be the MOST cariogenic carbohydrate? 2._____

   A. Starch B. Sucrose C. Glucose
   D. Glycogen E. Dextranase

3. Which of the following conditions is MOST suspect if a radiograph shows a dense, diffuse radiopacity at the apex of an endodontically treated mandibular left first molar? 3._____

   A. Osteoma B. Cementoma
   C. Dental granuloma D. Condensing osteitis
   E. Carcinoma

4. Which of the following conditions is associated with an alteration in the number of teeth? 4._____

   A. Cleidocranial dysostosis
   B. Achondroplastic dwarfism
   C. Juvenile diabetes
   D. Hypopituitarism
   E. Hypothyroidism

5. Which of the following restorative materials is the MOST radiolucent? 5._____

   A. Gutta-percha B. Dental amalgam
   C. Composite resin D. Zinc oxide-eugenol
   E. Methyl methacrylate

6. A soft tissue mass is present at the apex of a carious tooth. It is composed of fibrous connective tissue, dense in some areas and loose and vascular in others. There are focal aggregates of lymphocytes and plasmacytes and some neutrophils throughout. A few epithelial rests and viable bone spicules are present. 6._____
   The MOST likely diagnosis is

   A. radicular cyst B. central fibroma
   C. periapical abscess D. odontogenic fibroma
   E. periapical granuloma

7. Which of the following is characteristic of a primordial cyst? 7._____
   It

   A. develops in place of a tooth
   B. is attached to the apex of a tooth

C. is attached to the crown of a tooth
D. remains after the tooth is extracted
E. none of the above

8. The presence of a circulating antibody directed to intercellular cementing substance of stratified squamous epithelium is observed in 8.____

A. verruca vulgaris
B. bullous pemphigoid
C. pemphigus vulgaris
D. bullous lichen planus
E. dermatitis herpetiformis

9. Which of the following conditions is FREQUENTLY seen in pregnant patients? 9.____

A. Peripheral giant cell granuloma
B. Gingival fibrous hyperplasia
C. Gingival melanosis
D. Epulis fissuratum
E. Pyogenic granuloma

10. Which of the following lesions MOST commonly occur on the tongue? 10.____

A. Leiomyoma and myxoma
B. Hemangioma and mucocele
C. Rhabdomyoma and ossifying fibroma
D. Lipoma and central giant cell granuloma
E. Granular cell myoblastoma and lymphangioma

11. Which of the following intraoral neoplasms has the POOREST prognosis? 11.____

A. Verrucous carcinoma of the gingiva
B. Squamous cell carcinoma of the lip
C. Fibrosarcoma of the buccal mucosa
D. Melanoma of the alveolar ridge
E. Mixed tumor of the parotid gland

12. The prognosis is MOST favorable with carcinoma in the 12.____

A. tonsil
B. lower lip
C. hard palate
D. buccal mucosa
E. floor of the mouth

13. Which of the following dental disturbances will MOST likely be associated with the combined clinical findings of mobility, feeling of elongation and pain upon percussion of the affected tooth? 13.____

A. Acute alveolar abscess
B. Acute focal pulpitis
C. Periapical cyst
D. Periapical granuloma
E. None of the above

14. A 45-year-old female presents with a unilateral ache in the right ear which radiates to the angle of the mandible. There is a clicking noise in the right temporomandibular joint. Results of radiographs are negative. Palpation of the temporomandibular joint does not produce tenderness. The MOST probable clinical diagnosis is 14.____

A. ankylosis
B. osteoarthritis
C. traumatic arthritis
D. rheumatoid arthritis
E. myofascial pain dysfunction syndrome

15. Paget disease of bone is associated with a(n) 15.____

A. *elevated* serum amylase
B. *decreased* serum calcium
C. *elevated* serum acid phosphatase
D. *elevated* serum alkaline phosphatase
E. *decreased* serum alkaline phosphatase

16. Which of the following cysts will MOST often cause surgical hemorrhage? 16.____

A. Radicular
B. Follicular
C. Primordial
D. Traumatic bone
E. Aneurysmal bone

17. Which of the following MOST commonly involves only ONE bone? 17.____

A. Paget disease
B. Ossifying fibroma
C. Marble bone disease
D. Albright syndrome
E. All of the above

18. Which of the following is the MOST common developmental cyst? 18.____

A. Nasolabial
B. Median palatal
C. Globulomaxillary
D. Median mandibular
E. Nasopalatine duct

19. Which of the following diseases is characterized by palmar and plantar pits, keratinizing jaw cysts, and multiple skin cancers? 19.____

A. Ameloblastoma
B. Odontodysplasia
C. Costen syndrome
D. Gaucher disease
E. Multiple basal cell nevus syndrome

20. Which of the following non-oral diseases is associated with the GREATEST predisposition to oral squamous carcinoma? 20.____

A. Emphysema
B. Hyperthyroidism
C. Hepatic cirrhosis
D. Diabetes mellitus
E. Arteriosclerotic heart disease

21. Which of the following is the INITIAL response of the dental pulp to cavity preparation? 21.____

A. Vascular dilation
B. Acute inflammatory reaction
C. Infiltration by lymphocytes

D. Migration of odontoblastic nuclei
E. Migration of odontoblasts from the cell rich zone

22. Intrinsic staining of enamel may be caused by each of the following EXCEPT 22.____

A. porphyria
B. endemic fluorosis
C. tetracycline therapy
D. amelogenesis imperfecta
E. erythroblastosis fetalis

23. Multiple myeloma is associated with all of the following EXCEPT 23.____

A. bone pain
B. Bence Jones proteinuria
C. osteoblastic bone lesions
D. myeloma cells in bone marrow
E. none of the above

24. Radiographs of an asymptomatic 19-year-old patient disclose a well-demarcated, bilocu- 24.____
lated 3x2 cm. radio-lucency in the mandibular molar area.
Each of the following should be included in the differential diagnosis EXCEPT

A. ameloblastoma
B. cementoblastoma
C. traumatic bone cyst
D. odontogenic keratocyst
E. central giant cell granuloma

25. Each of the following is a symptom of a malignant mixed tumor of the parotid gland EXCEPT 25.____

A. paresthesia of the upper lip
B. swelling in the parotid area
C. drooping of the commissure
D. fixation to underlying structures
E. ulceration of the cornea of the eye

KEY (CORRECT ANSWERS)

1.	C	11.	D
2.	B	12.	B
3.	D	13.	A
4.	A	14.	E
5.	E	15.	D
6.	E	16.	E
7.	A	17.	B
8.	C	18.	E
9.	E	19.	E
10.	E	20.	C

21. D
22. D
23. C
24. B
25. E

ORAL PATHOLOGY / RADIOGRAPHY

EXAMINATION SECTION
TEST 1

DIRECTIONS: Each question or incomplete statement is followed by several suggested answers or completions. Select the one that BEST answers the question or completes the statement. *PRINT THE LETTER OF THE CORRECT ANSWER IN THE SPACE AT THE RIGHT.*

1. Which of the following may interfere with proper healing of a wound? 1.____

   A. Avitaminosis C
   B. Hypoproteinemia
   C. Therapeutic doses of cortisone
   D. All of the above
   E. None of the above

2. Which of the following periapical lesions is a sequela of pulpal pathosis? 2.____

   A. Hypercementosis
   B. Ossifying fibroma
   C. Condensing osteitis
   D. Benign cementoblastoma
   E. Simple (traumatic) bone cyst

3. Which of the following cysts occurs in an extraosseous location? 3.____

   A. Nasolabial
   B. Nasopalatine
   C. Median palatal
   D. Globulomaxillary
   E. Radicular

4. If multiple myeloma is suspected because of a patient's medical history and intraoral radiographs, which radio-graphic projection is BEST to confirm the suspected diagnosis? 4.____

   A. Lateral skull
   B. Lateral oblique
   C. Anterior-posterior
   D. Posterior-anterior
   E. Temporomandibular survey

5. Which sites are characteristically affected in Stevens-Johnson syndrome? 5.____

   A. Liver, spleen, pancreas
   B. Conjunctiva, genitalia, oral mucosa
   C. Oral mucosa, lacrimal apparatus, ears
   D. Parotid gland, palate, submaxillary gland
   E. Conjunctiva, oral mucosa, ears

6. An IMMEDIATE biopsy should be performed on 6.____

   A. an ulceration of 6 days' duration
   B. many small, yellow papules on the buccal mucosa
   C. a white patch of 20 years' duration in a 20-year-old man
   D. an indurated, 1 cm. mass on the lateral border of the tongue
   E. an erythematous patch of 10 days' duration associated with a recent burn

7. Which of the following cysts is lined with stratified squamous epithelium or columnar epithelium and has blood vessels, nerves, and mucous glands in the walls? 7.____

   A. Dermoid
   B. Periapical
   C. Median mandibular
   D. Nasopalatine duct
   E. Nasolabial

8. Which of the following lesions is actually an overabundance of granulation tissue? 8.____

   A. Giant cell lesion
   B. Epulis fissuratum
   C. Pyogenic granuloma
   D. Irritation fibroma
   E. Hypertrophic hemangioma

9. Which of the following is the MOST effective aid to detecting incipient proximal caries on the mesial surface of a maxillary lateral incisor? 9.____

   A. A dental explorer
   B. Direct visualization
   C. Panoramic radiograph
   D. Bite-wing radiograph
   E. Periapical radiograph

10. Dermal and oral manifestations are observed MOST commonly in _______ leukemia. 10.____

   A. monocytic
   B. myelocytic
   C. lymphocytic
   D. aleukemic
   E. all of the above

11. Which of the following is CONTRAINDICATED in managing craniofacial fibrous dysplasia? 11.____

   A. Curettage
   B. Bloc excision
   C. Radiation therapy
   D. Surgical recontouring
   E. Close observation only

12. Hairy tongue is characterized by hypertrophy of the _______ papillae. 12.____

   A. foliate
   B. filiform
   C. fungiform
   D. circumvallate
   E. none of the above

13. Which of the following diseases is characterized by microscopic suprabasal intraepithelial bullae and acantholysis? 13.____

   A. Pemphigus vulgaris
   B. Erythema multiforme
   C. Lupus erythematosus
   D. Periadenitis mucosa necrotica recurrens
   E. None of the above

14. In myofascial pain dysfunction syndrome, which muscle is MOST apt to exhibit tenderness? 14.____

   A. Masseter
   B. Temporal is
   C. Medial pterygoid
   D. Lateral pterygoid
   E. Sternocleidomastoid

15. The induction effect is characteristic of which of the following lesions? 15.____

   A. Myxofibroma
   B. Ameloblastoma
   C. Cementoblastoma

D. Ameloblastic fibro-odontoma
E. Odontogenic adenomatoid tumor

16. Bilateral mandibular involvement is characteristic of 16.____

A. osteoma
B. cherubism
C. ameloblastoma
D. monostotic fibrous dysplasia
E. central giant cell granuloma

17. *Burning tongue* may be a symptom of 17.____

A. neurosis
B. diabetes mellitus
C. pernicious anemia
D. vitamin B complex deficiency
E. any of the above

18. Which of the following conditions may show evidence of pigmentation? 18.____

I. Cherubism
II. Peutz-Jeghers syndrome
III. Addison disease
IV. Albright syndrome
V. Paget disease of bone

The CORRECT answer is:

A. I, II, III, IV
B. I, II, IV, V
C. I, III, IV
D. I, IV, V
E. II, III, IV

19. Which of the following conditions are known to promote or increase dental caries? 19.____

I. A reduction in the flow of saliva
II. The presence of streptococcal organisms in the oral cavity
III. Increased viscosity of saliva
IV. An increase in dietary sugars
V. Vitamin B and C deficiencies

The CORRECT answer is:

A. I, II, III, IV
B. I, II, IV
C. I, III
D. II, IV, V
E. All ofthe above

20. Which of the following tumors may arise in the parotid salivary gland? 20.____

I. Oncocytoma
II. Mixed tumor
III. Adenocarcinoma
IV. Warthin tumor
V. Mucoepidermoid tumor

The CORRECT answer is:

A. I, II, III
B. I, III, V
C. II, IV, V
D. III, IV, V
E. All of the above

21. Supernumerary teeth are characteristic of 21.____

I. cleidocranial dysostosis
II. ectodermal dysplasia
III. Gardner syndrome
IV. Romberg disease

The CORRECT answer is:

A. I *only*
B. I, II
C. I, III
D. I, IV
E. II, III

22. Metastases RARELY occur from 22.____

I. ameloblastoma
II. verrucous carcinoma
III. basal cell carcinoma
IV. adenoid cystic carcinoma

The CORRECT answer is:

A. I, II
B. I, II, III
C. I, III
D. I, III, IV
E. II, III, IV

23. A tooth associated with which of the following conditions would fail to respond to vitality tests? 23.____

I. Periapical granuloma
II. Periapical cyst
III. Chronic periapical abscess
IV. Condensing osteitis
V. Pulpal congestion

The CORRECT answer is:

A. I, II, III, IV
B. I, II, III, V
C. I, II, IV, V
D. I, III, IV, V
E. II, III, IV, V

24. A 47-year-old woman complains that her maxillary denture does not fit. Examination reveals unilateral enlargement of an edentulous maxilla. Intraoral radiographs of the involved area shown an abnormal trabeculation with a *ground glass* appearance. Further tests should include 24.____

A. C.B.C. and SMA 12/60
B. serum cholesterol and creatinine values
C. wrist radiographs and basal metabolic rate
D. skull radiograph and blood chemistries
E. basal metabolic rate and creatinine values

25. Tooth vitality is determined radiographically by the 25.____

A. presence of secondary dentin
B. closeness of decay to the pulp
C. normal appearance of tooth tissues
D. presence of a periapical radiolucency
E. none of the above

KEY (CORRECT ANSWERS)

1. D
2. C
3. A
4. A
5. B
6. D
7. D
8. C
9. E
10. A
11. C
12. B
13. A
14. D
15. D
16. B
17. E
18. E
19. A
20. E
21. C
22. B
23. A
24. D
25. E

TEST 2

DIRECTIONS: Each question or incomplete statement is followed by several suggested answers or completions. Select the one that BEST answers the question or completes the statement. *PRINT THE LETTER OF THE CORRECT ANSWER IN THE SPACE AT THE RIGHT.*

1. Which of the following cysts are USUALLY associated with vital teeth? 1.____
   I. Dentigerous cysts
   II. Lateral periodontal cysts
   III. Odontogenic keratocysts
   IV. Globulomaxillary cysts
   V. Radicular cysts

   The CORRECT answer is:

   A. I, II, III, IV
   B. I, II, III, V
   C. I, II, IV, V
   D. I, III, IV, V
   E. II, III, IV, V

2. COMMON sites of intraoral squamous cell carcinoma include the 2.____
   I. hard palate
   II. tongue
   III. gingiva
   IV. labial mucosa
   V. floor of the mouth

   The CORRECT answer is:

   A. I, II, III
   B. I, III
   C. II, III, IV
   D. II, IV
   E. II, V

3. Squamous cell carcinoma of the tongue has been related etiologically to 3.____
   I. syphilitic glossitis
   II. Plummer-Vinson syndrome
   III. hepatitis A
   IV. Mikulicz syndrome

   The CORRECT answer is:

   A. I, II
   B. I, IV
   C. II, III
   D. III, IV
   E. All of the above

4. An INCREASED incidence of osteosarcoma is expected in bone affected by 4.____
   I. cherubism
   II. polyostotic fibrous dysplasia
   III. Paget disease
   IV. osteopetrosis

   The CORRECT answer is:

   A. I, II
   B. I, III
   C. I, IV
   D. II, III
   E. II, IV

5. Kilovoltage influences the x-ray beam and the radiograph by 5.____
   I. decreasing film density
   II. altering contrast quality
   III. determining the quality of x-rays produced
   IV. determining the velocity of electrons to the anode
   V. producing soft rays with good penetrating qualities

   The CORRECT answer is:

   A. I, III, IV
   B. I, IV, V
   C. II, III, IV
   D. II, III, V
   E. II, IV, V

6. The preservative GENERALLY used for a biopsied specimen is 6.____

   A. acetone
   B. alcohol
   C. xylocaine
   D. Zenker's solution
   E. 10 percent formalin

7. The characteristic hue of the crowns of teeth with internal resorption is due to 7.____

   A. degeneration and necrosis of the pulp tissue
   B. peculiar changes in the consistency of dentin
   C. the presence of hyperplastic vascular pulp tissue
   D. deposition of pigment in the odontoblastic layer
   E. an optical phenomenon related to the difference in refractive indices of normal and affected areas

8. The oral tissues MOST sensitive to x-ray irradiation are the 8.____

   A. developing tooth buds and the salivary glands
   B. gingival epithelium and the maxillary cortical bone
   C. alveolar crestal bone and the mandibular nerve
   D. intrinsic tongue muscle and the maxillary sinus epithelium
   E. periodontal ligament and hair follicles of the lower lip

9. Of the following infections, the one MOST likely to result in a chronic suppurative lesion about the jaws is 9.____

   A. candidiasis
   B. actinomycosis
   C. blastomycosis
   D. histoplasmosis
   E. none of the above

10. For five days, a 25-year-old man has had painful oral ulcerations. Several reddish macular lesions are present on his face and hands, most of which have a ring-like or bull's eye appearance. He had *cold sores* two weeks earlier. 10.____

    Tentative diagnosis is

    A. lichen planus
    B. aphthous ulcers
    C. pityriasis rosea
    D. verruca vulgaris
    E. erythema multiforme

11. The oral manifestations of Peutz-Jeghers syndrome include 11.____

    A. multiple papillomas
    B. gingival hyperplasia
    C. sebaceous glands in the oral mucosa

D. silver pigmentation of the oral mucosa
E. none of the above

12. An elderly patient who is anemic complains of back pain. Numerous circumscribed radiolucencies are evident on a panoramic film. This patient should be suspected of having 12.____

A. Ewing sarcoma
B. chondrosarcoma
C. multiple myeloma
D. Letterer-Siwe disease
E. diabetes mellitus

13. The x-ray beam is filtered to 13.____

A. soften the beam
B. restrict the beam size
C. remove long wavelength x-rays
D. remove short wavelength x-rays
E. none of the above

14. Proliferation of multinucleated giant cells, histiocytes, fibroblasts, and capillaries occurring about a fragment of suture material embedded in the oral mucosa is a 14.____

A. cicatrix
B. cellulitis
C. pyogenic granuloma
D. giant cell granuloma
E. foreign body granuloma

15. The clinical appearance and the texture of a beginning carcinoma of the floor of the mouth is 15.____

A. red and soft
B. white and rough
C. red and rough
D. either A or B
E. neither A nor B

16. Chronic fluoride intoxication is characterized by 16.____

A. extensive arthritic changes in the spine, producing rigidity
B. calcification of muscles and tendon sheaths
C. marked osteosclerosis
D. all of the above
E. none of the above

17. A 65-year-old man has an ulcerated, 3 cm. lesion on the lateral border of the tongue. The recommended procedure for making a diagnosis is to 17.____

A. excise the entire lesion
B. perform an incisional biopsy
C. take a cytologic smear of the ulcerated area
D. none of the above
E. any of the above

18. The etiology of multiple neurofibromatosis is 18.____

A. genetic
B. a virus
C. an injury
D. an endocrine dysfunction
E. bacterial

19. The speed with which electrons travel from the filament of the cathode to the target of the anode depends upon the 19.____

A. potential difference between the two electrodes
B. number of milliamperes in the tube circuit
C. angle between the filament and the target
D. voltage in the filament circuit
E. size of the electron cloud

20. Physical examination of a 28-year-old man reveals an extensive, smooth enlargement of the body of the mandible in the molar region. The patient states that the enlargement has been present for two years and has slowly and steadily increased in size. 20.____
The MOST probable clinical diagnosis is

A. osteosarcoma
B. ameloblastoma
C. osteomyelitis
D. osteitis deformans
E. osteoma

21. A cementoma DIFFERS from a periapical granuloma in that a cementoma 21.____

A. shows radiopacity in its early stages, and the involved tooth is vital
B. begins as an apical osteolytic lesion, and the involved tooth is vital
C. is a harmless lesion, and occurs most frequently in the premolar region
D. has a history of trauma, and in its latest stages shows as a radiolucent area
E. begins as an apical osteolytic lesion and the involved tooth is nonvital

22. The rationale for surgical removal and biopsy of a large periapical lesion suspected to be of inflammatory origin is that 22.____

A. a granuloma contains epithelial cells capable of cyst formation
B. fibrous tissue in a granuloma may retard bone formation
C. a neoplasm is likely to originate from the epithelium in a cyst or a granuloma
D. pus in a granuloma may cause eventual failure
E. clinical diagnosis can be confirmed microscopically

23. The feature that FREQUENTLY distinguishes herpes zoster from other vesiculobullous eruptions is 23.____

A. unilateral occurrence
B. severe, burning pain
C. prominent crusting of lesions
D. seasonal pattern of development
E. subepidermal bullous formation

24. Occlusal radiographs are useful in locating 24.____

A. the hyoid bone
B. the mental foramen
C. maxillary sinus mucoceles
D. sialoliths in Stensen's duct
E. sialoliths in Wharton's duct

25. The MOST frequent stimulating factor in the occurrence of a pyogenic granuloma is 25.____

A. puberty
B. pregnancy
C. a large carious lesion
D. streptococcal microorganisms
E. a local irritant, such as calculus

KEY (CORRECT ANSWERS)

1. A
2. E
3. A
4. D
5. C

6. E
7. C
8. A
9. B
10. E

11. E
12. C
13. C
14. E
15. D

16. D
17. B
18. A
19. A
20. B

21. B
22. E
23. A
24. E
25. E

TEST 3

DIRECTIONS: Each question or incomplete statement is followed by several suggested answers or completions. Select the one that BEST answers the question or completes the statement. *PRINT THE LETTER OF THE CORRECT ANSWER IN THE SPACE AT THE RIGHT.*

1. From clinical observations, caries of the dentin that is relatively light in color indicates 1.____

   A. slow progression
   B. rapid progression
   C. rapid enamel decalcification
   D. the presence of enamel lamellae
   E. rapid secondary dent in formation

2. An x-ray beam is heterogeneous or polychromatic because 2.____

   A. the potential across the tube changes constantly as the AC voltage varies
   B. the temperature of the filament varies causing a variation in the number of electrons in the electron cloud
   C. the aluminum filter absorbs photons on a random basis
   D. it belongs to the family of electromagnetic radiations
   E. the potential across the tube remains constant as the AC voltage varies

3. The single MOST effective means of reducing patient radiation dose to intraoral tissues is to use 3.____

   A. a lead apron
   B. high-speed film
   C. increased filtration
   D. intensifying screens
   E. increased target-film distance

4. The EARLIEST common symptom of acute pulpitis secondary to a carious lesion is 4.____

   A. continuous pain
   B. aerodontalgia
   C. tooth discoloration
   D. thermal sensitivity
   E. pain on percussion

5. To avoid exposure to secondary radiation when taking radiographs, the dentist should stand 5.____

   A. in back of the patient
   B. next to the patient
   C. at least three feet from the patient
   D. at least six feet from the source of secondary radiation
   E. ten feet from the patient

6. Exophthalmos, nervousness, tachycardia, heat intolerance, and hypertension are indicative of 6.____

   A. hypothyroidism
   B. hyperthyroidism
   C. hypoparathyroidism
   D. hyperparathyroidism
   E. pseudohypoparathyroidism

7. Examination of a 3-year-old boy reveals a fracture of his right leg, blue sclera, deafness, and a peculiarly shaped head. Opalescent dentin is found in many of his primary teeth. The MOST probable clinical diagnosis is 7.____

A. osteopetrosis
B. Marfan syndrome
C. osteogenesis imperfecta
D. cleidocranial dysostosis
E. infantile cortical hyperostosis

8. A patient receives a tenative diagnosis of central giant cell granuloma. For definitive diagnosis, serum calcium level should be determined to distinguish between granuloma and 8.____

A. osteopetrosis
B. fibrous dysplasia
C. hyperparathyroidism
D. osteogenesis imperfecta
E. Paget disease of bone

9. An autoantibody directed to the basement membrane of stratified squamous epithelium is a feature of 9.____

A. pemphigus vulgaris
B. white sponge nevus
C. erythema multiforme
D. dermatitis herpetiformis
E. mucous membrane pemphigoid

10. Certain cariogenic strains of streptococci have the ability to metabolize dietary sucrose and produce a sticky, slimy gel that is insoluble and adheres tenaciously to teeth. This substance is 10.____

A. mucin
B. plaque
C. dextran
D. lactic acid
E. protein factor

11. A well-circumscribed, white patch in the mandibular facial sulcus appears secondary to placing aspirin in the area. The MOST probable diagnosis is ______ of the oral mucosa. 11.____

A. hyperkeratosis
B. hyperplasia
C. hypertrophy
D. necrosis
E. none of the above

12. A symmetrically widened periodontal ligament space around one or two adjacent teeth is reported to be the EARLIEST radiographic sign of 12.____

A. osteosarcoma
B. osteitis deformans
C. florid osseous dysplasia
D. sclerosing cemental masses
E. craniofacial fibrous dysplasia

13. Examination of a 79-year-old man reveals a 3 cm., flat, mottled, brown-black splotchy lesion on the left side of his face. The margins of the lesion are not palpable. The patient states that the lesion has been increasing in size for ten years.
The MOST likely diagnosis is 13.____

A. *age spot*
B. lentigo maligna
C. nodular melanoma
D. junctional nevus
E. superficial spreading melanoma

14. An intense lymphocytic infiltration of one or more major salivary glands with replacement of acinar structures that is often associated with keratoconjunctivitis and autoimmune disorders is characteristic of ______ syndrome. 14.____

A. Apert
B. Fanconi
C. Sjögren
D. Goltz-Gorlin
E. Melkersson-Rosenthal

15. If a dried radiograph were processed a second time, its appearance would show 15.____

A. *increased* contrast and density
B. *decreased* contrast and density
C. *increased* contrast *only*
D. *increased* density *only*
E. *no change* in contrast or density

16. The MOST common site of intraoral minor salivary gland neoplasms is the 16.____

A. lip
B. cheek
C. palate
D. tongue
E. retromolar area

17. The density of a radiograph is reduced by increasing 17.____

A. kilovoltage
B. milliamperage
C. exposure time
D. source-film distance
E. diameter of the aperture

18. A form of inflammatory hyperplasia that occurs in the palate and is associated with ill-fitting dentures and poor oral hygiene is 18.____

A. palatal torus
B. denture sore spot
C. denture sore mouth
D. epulis fissuratum
E. palatal papillomatosis

19. The component of developer that gives detail to the radio-graphic image is 19.____

A. hydroquinone
B. sodium sulfite
C. sodium carbonate
D. potassium bromide
E. none of the above

20. Ameloblastomas MOST commonly occur between the ages of 20.____

A. 1 and 10
B. 10 and 20
C. 20 and 40
D. 40 and 60
E. 60 and 70

21. The odontogenic cyst having the HIGHEST recurrence rate is the 21.____

A. radicular cyst
B. periapical cyst
C. keratocyst
D. dentigerous cyst
E. dental lamina cyst of the newborn

22. Obliteration of pulp chambers and root canals in BOTH primary and permanent teeth is characteristic of 22.____

A. shell teeth
B. endemic fluorosis
C. enamel hypoplasia
D. amelogenesis imperfecta
E. dentinogenesis imperfecta

23. A patient received a palatal injection of a local anesthetic before extraction of a second premolar. Seventy-two hours later, the patient has a 1.5 cm. ulcer covered by a gray-white slough at the injection site. 23.____
The MOST probable cause of this lesion is

A. aspirin burn
B. introduction of a foreign body
C. infection induced by needle contamination
D. infarction secondary to vasoconstrictor-induced anoxia
E. none of the above

24. Which of the following groups of permanent teeth shows LEAST caries incidence? 24.____

A. Maxillary second premolars
B. Mandibular second premolars
C. Maxillary and mandibular first molars
D. Maxillary central and lateral incisors
E. Mandibular central and lateral incisors

25. Which of the following is LEAST likely to occur as a primary neoplasm within the jaw bones? 25.____

A. Osteoma
B. Mixed tumor
C. Multiple myeloma
D. Osteogenic sarcoma
E. All of the above

KEY (CORRECT ANSWERS)

1. B
2. A
3. B
4. D
5. D

6. B
7. C
8. C
9. E
10. C

11. D
12. A
13. B
14. C
15. E

16. C
17. D
18. E
19. A
20. C

21. C
22. E
23. D
24. E
25. B

ORAL PATHOLOGY / RADIOGRAPHY

EXAMINATION SECTION
TEST 1

DIRECTIONS: Each question or incomplete statement is followed by several suggested answers or completions. Select the one that BEST answers the question or completes the statement. *PRINT THE LETTER OF THE CORRECT ANSWER IN THE SPACE AT THE RIGHT.*

1. A radiograph shows an unerupted mandibular third molar with a 3 cm. pericoronal radiolucency. 1.____
   The MOST likely diagnosis is

   A. primordial cyst
   B. dentigerous cyst
   C. latent bone cyst
   D. simple bone cyst
   E. ameloblastoma

2. A 15-year-old boy has multiple vesiculating oral ulcers, severe pain, malaise, lymphadenopathy, and an oral temperature of 103°F. of three days' duration. 2.____
   The MOST likely diagnosis is

   A. herpes zoster
   B. cat scratch fever
   C. periadenitis aphthae
   D. infectious mononucleosis
   E. acute herpetic gingivostomatitis

3. Image sharpness on a radiograph is INCREASED by 3.____

   A. using a small focal spot size
   B. using a large focal spot size
   C. increasing object-film distance
   D. decreasing target-skin distance
   E. both A and D

4. Nicotine stomatitis is characterized by 4.____

   A. ulceration of the tonsillar crypt
   B. an inflamed orifice of Stenson's duct
   C. local exfoliation of filiform papillae
   D. ulceration of the inner surface of the lip
   E. inflamed orifices of palatal mucous glands

5. An extracted molar has a mass of soft tissue attached to one root. On microscopic examination, this tissue is found to consist of fairly dense, fibrous connective tissue with many lymphocytes, plasma cells, and capillaries. The MOST probable diagnosis is 5.____

   A. fibroma
   B. hemangioma
   C. radicular cyst
   D. dental granuloma
   E. fibrous healing defect (scar)

6. Of the following tissues, the MOST sensitive to radiation is 6.____

   A. lymphoid B. muscle C. bone
   D. skin E. any of the above

7. A 5-year-old boy has symmetric, bilateral enlargement of posterior jaws. Radiographic examination reveals multi-ocular radiolucencies of the jaws. His father reports that he had a similar condition. 7.____
   The MOST likely diagnosis is

   A. cherubism
   B. Albright syndrome
   C. hyperparathyroidism
   D. cleidocranial dysostosis
   E. juvenile Paget disease of bone

8. Advanced basal cell carcinoma FREQUENTLY involves normal tissue by spreading by way of 8.____

   A. arteries B. lymphatics
   C. nerve sheaths D. marrow spaces
   E. direct extension

9. A high school football player using a protective mouth guard has crepitation in the left temporomandibular joint, a trigger zone of tenderness in the left temporalis musculature, and stiffness of the jaw on wakening. 9.____
   The MOST likely diagnosis is

   A. tic douloureux
   B. myofascial pain syndrome
   C. atypical facial neuralgia
   D. arthritis of the temporomandibular joint
   E. none of the above

10. Hypercementosis is often found in association with 10.____

   A. hyperparathyroidism
   B. a giant cell granuloma
   C. a cementifying fibroma
   D. Paget disease of bone
   E. polyostotic fibrous dysplasia

11. If correct developing time for a film is *X*, MINIMAL fixing time is _______ X. 11.____

   A. 1/2 B. 1 C. 2 D. 3 E. 4

12. The density of a radiograph is REDUCED by increasing 12.____

   A. kilovoltage B. milliamperage
   C. exposure time D. source-film distance
   E. diameter of the aperture

13. A patient exhibits marked attrition of primary and permanent teeth; radiographs reveal a marked tendency toward obliteration of many pulp canals. The patient's mother and brother also have histories of this condition. The MOST likely diagnosis is 13.____

A. mottled enamel
B. enamel hypoplasia
C. enamel hypomaturation
D. dentinogenesis imperfecta
E. none of the above

14. The purpose of collimating an x-ray beam is to 14.____

A. reduce the size of the beam to facilitate easier visualization of the central ray
B. avoid delivering unnecessary radiation to the patient
C. remove the less penetrating x-ray photons
D. reduce exposure time
E. all of the above

15. The microscopic appearance of a congenital epulis of the newborn MOST closely resembles a(n) 15.____

A. Fordyce spot
B. mixed tumor
C. epithelial pearl
D. peripheral giant cell granuloma
E. granular cell tumor (myoblastoma)

16. A young man complains of malaise, urtications, and large, painful and bloody, ulcerobullous lesions on his lips and oral mucosa. The lip lesions are black and encrusted. The MOST likely diagnosis is 16.____

A. pemphigus vegetans
B. pemphigus vulgaris
C. erythema multiforme
D. bullous lichen planus
E. benign mucous membrane pemphigoid

17. Odontogenic adenomatoid tumors occur MOST often in the 17.____

A. anterior maxilla
B. posterior maxilla
C. anterior mandible
D. posterior mandible
E. maxillary sinus

18. The MOST common malignancy in the oral cavity is ______ carcinoma. 18.____

A. metastatic
B. basal cell
C. epidermoid
D. mucoepidermoid
E. adenoid cystic

19. The quantity of electrons available for x-rays is determined PRIMARILY by 19.____

A. kilovoltage setting
B. amount of filtration
C. degree of collimation
D. milliamperage setting
E. none of the above

20. Verrucous carcinoma COMMONLY appears as a(n) 20.____

A. crater-like ulceration
B. white, ulcerated patch
C. red, velvet patch
D. exophytic mass
E. none of the above

21. A necrotizing, ragged mucosal ulceration with no apparent inflammatory response is indicative of 21.____

A. leukocytosis
B. agranulocytosis
C. polycythemia vera
D. sickle cell anemia
E. infectious mononucleosis

22. An ameloblastoma is MOST likely to develop from the epithelial lining of which of the following cysts? 22.____

A. Residual
B. Periapical
C. Dentigerous
D. Nasopalatine duct
E. Lateral periodontal

23. Which of the following is characteristic of a primordial cyst? 23.____
It

A. develops in place of a tooth
B. attaches to the apex of a tooth
C. attaches to the crown of a tooth
D. remains after the tooth is extracted
E. none of the above

24. Which of the following dental disturbances is associated with the combined clinical findings of mobility and feeling of elongation and pain upon percussion of the affected tooth? 24.____

A. Periapical cyst
B. Acute focal pulpitis
C. Periapical granuloma
D. Acute alveolar abscess
E. Radicular cyst

25. Which of the following syndromes is associated with predisposition to oral and pharyngeal carcinoma? 25.____

A. Gardner
B. Sjögren
C. Gushing
D. Peutz-Jeghers
E. Plummer-Vinson

KEY (CORRECT ANSWERS)

1. B
2. E
3. A
4. E
5. D

6. A
7. A
8. E
9. B
10. D

11. C
12. D
13. D
14. B
15. E

16. C
17. A
18. C
19. D
20. D

21. B
22. C
23. A
24. D
25. E

TEST 2

DIRECTIONS: Each question or incomplete statement is followed by several suggested answers or completions. Select the one that BEST answers the question or completes the statement. *PRINT THE LETTER OF THE CORRECT ANSWER IN THE SPACE AT THE RIGHT.*

1. Degeneration of the myelin sheaths of peripheral nerves in a diabetic may be manifested intraorally by 1.____

   A. causalgia and neuralgia
   B. acanthosis and acantholysis
   C. vesicle and ulcer formation
   D. glossopyrosis and glossodynia
   E. causalgia and ulcer formation

2. An air-water spray syringe is being used to clear debris while treating a deep periodontal pocket on the facial surface of a maxillary first molar. Suddenly, the patient' s face swells on the affected side. The swelling is painless and bubbly to palpation. 2.____
   The MOST likely diagnosis is

   A. traumatic hematoma
   B. soft tissue emphysema
   C. allergy to the epinephrine cord
   D. rupture of the pterygoid plexus
   E. none of the above

3. The Committee on Radiation Protection of the National Bureau of Standards recommends that a person who works near radiation be exposed in any one year to a MAXIMUM dose of ______ rem. 3.____

   A. 1 B. 3 C. 5 D. 8 E. 10

4. In general, intraoral radiography requires a GREATER skin exposure than extraoral radiography because 4.____

   A. a smaller focal spot is used in intraoral radiography
   B. saliva attenuates the primary beam in intraoral radiography
   C. intensifying screens are used in extraoral radiography
   D. scattered radiation enhances the image in extraoral radiography
   E. all of the above

5. Dental plaque is composed PRIMARILY of water and 5.____
   I. bacteria
   II. extracellular matrix
   III. desquamated epithelial cells
   IV. food debris
   The CORRECT answer is:

   A. I, II B. I, III C. II, III
   D. III, IV E. All of the above

6. In the acidogenic theory, the components that play a role in dental caries include 6.____
   I. carbohydrates
   II. proteins
   III. acids
   IV. bacteria
   V. lipids

   The CORRECT answer is:

   A. I, II, III B. I, II, IV C. I, II, V
   D. I, III, IV E. I, III, V

7. Management of inflammatory hyperplasia (epulis fissuratum) resulting from denture irritation includes 7.____
   I. antifungal therapy
   II. surgical removal of hyperplastic tissue
   III. microscopic examination of altered tissue
   IV. construction of new dentures or denture bases

   The CORRECT answer is:

   A. I, II, III B. I, II, IV C. I, III, IV
   D. II, III E. II, III, IV

8. The aluminum filter in the x-ray tubehead functions to 8.____
   I. *reduce* exposure to patients' skin
   II. *absorb* long-wavelength photons preferentially
   III. *absorb* short-wavelength photons preferentially
   IV. *increase* penetrating qualities of the beam
   V. *decrease* penetrating qualities of the beam

   The CORRECT answer is:

   A. I, II B. I, II, IV C. I, II, V
   D. I, III, V E. III, IV

9. A 50-year-old woman has a swelling of the lateral aspect of the left side of the neck. The lesion has been present for six months; within the last two months, the lesion increased in size and is now painful. Examination reveals a 0.5 cm. ulceration of skin overlying the mass. There is notable distortion of the midfacial region when the patient speaks. 9.____
   This symptom complex is suggestive of
   I. adenoid cystic carcinoma
   II. pleomorphic adenoma
   III. oxyphilic adenoma (oncocytoma)
   IV. malignant mixed tumor
   V. papillary cystadenoma lymphomatosum (Warthin tumor)

   The CORRECT answer is:

   A. I, IV B. I, V C. II, III, V
   D. II, IV E. IV, V

10. Which of the following should be considered in the differential diagnosis of a well-defined radiolucency at the apex of an endodontically treated tooth that received periapical surgery three years ago? 10.____

I. Osteoma
II. Apical scar
III. Periapical cyst
IV. Dental granuloma
V. Central giant cell granuloma

The CORRECT answer is:

A. I, II, III, IV
B. I, III
C. I, IV
D. II, III, IV, V
E. II, III, V

11. Which of the following are COMMON features of an ameloblastoma? It 11.____

I. is found most often in the mandibular third molar region
II. is found most often in the maxillary canine region
III. occurs most often in persons under 20 years of age
IV. has a high recurrence rate following curettage
V. frequently metastasizes

The CORRECT answer is:

A. I, III
B. I, IV
C. I, IV, V
D. II, III
E. II, IV, V

12. Which of the following REDUCE the amount of radiation to a patient? 12.____

I. Using a high speed film
II. Using an aluminum filter
III. Using low kVp
IV. Increasing target-film distance
V. Decreasing target-film distance

The CORRECT answer is:

A. I, II
B. I, II, III, IV
C. I, II, IV
D. I, III, V
E. II, III, IV

13. A glossitis that predisposes to development of squamous cell carcinoma is associated with 13.____

I. vitamin B_{12} deficiency
II. iron deficiency
III. syphilis
IV. nicotine stomatitis
V. sickle cell anemia

The CORRECT answer is:

A. I, II
B. I, IV, V
C. II, III
D. III, IV
E. IV, V

14. Chronic exposure to sunlight has been implicated in the pathogenesis of 14.____

I. basal cell carcinoma
II. lymphoepithelioma
III. junctional nevus
IV. verruca vulgaris
V. carcinoma of the lip

The CORRECT answer is:

A. I *only*
B. I, III, V
C. I, V
D. III, IV, V
E. III, V

15. Which of the following cysts MOST often causes surgical hemorrhaging? 15.____

A. Radicular
B. Follicular
C. Primordial
D. Traumatic bone
E. Aneurysmal bone

16. Which of the following is the MOST frequent cause of ankylosis of the temporomandibular joint? 16.____

A. Osteoarthritis
B. Traumatic injury
C. Congenital syphilis
D. Traumatic occlusion
E. Metastatic malignancy

17. Erosive lichen planus involving the gingiva is clinically similar to 17.____

A. monilial gingivitis
B. desquamative gingivitis
C. herpetic gingivostomatitis
D. necrotizing ulcerative gingivitis
E. none of the above

18. Which of the following is a hereditary disorder characterized by development of rachitic-like deformities, an absence of cementum, enlargement of pulp chambers, and premature loss of primary teeth? 18.____

A. Acromegaly
B. Gaucher disease
C. Hypophosphatasia
D. Niemann-Pick disease
E. Hypophosphatemia (vitamin D-resistant rickets)

19. Incisional biopsy is CONTRAINDICATED for which of the following benign neoplasms? 19.____

A. Lipoma
B. Osteoma
C. Fibroma
D. Melanoma
E. Hemangioma

20. When treated with simple curettage, which odontogenic tumor is MOST likely to recur? 20.____

A. Complex odontoma
B. Compound odontoma
C. Odontogenic myxoma
D. Ameloblastic fibroma
E. Odontogenic adenomatoid tumor

21. Which of the following conditions may be histologically misdiagnosed as a benign lesion? 21.____

A. Lentigo maligna
B. Lymphoepithelioma
C. Verrucous carcinoma
D. Basal cell carcinoma
E. Adenoid cystic carcinoma

22. Which of the following types of malignancy may arise from Paget disease of bone? 22.____

A. Sarcoma
B. Leukemia
C. Adenocarcinoma
D. Squamous cell carcinoma
E. None of the above

23. Diabetes insipidus, exophthalmos, and radiolucent bone defects within the skull are MOST suggestive of 23.____

A. sickle cell anemia
B. Niemann-Pick disease
C. Letterer-Siwe disease
D. Hand-Schüller-Christian disease
E. Addison's disease

24. How should PROPER subject contrast be maintained when taking a radiograph of a patient with thick, hypercalcified jaws? 24.____

A. Increase mA
B. Increase kVp
C. Use a high-contrast film
D. Increase exposure time
E. Increase development time

25. The MOST common site for formation of a pyogenic granuloma is the 25.____

A. tongue
B. palate
C. gingiva
D. buccal mucosa
E. floor of the mouth

KEY (CORRECT ANSWERS)

1. D
2. B
3. C
4. C
5. A

6. D
7. E
8. B
9. A
10. D

11. B
12. C
13. C
14. C
15. E

16. B
17. B
18. C
19. E
20. C

21. E
22. A
23. D
24. B
25. C

TEST 3

DIRECTIONS: Each question or incomplete statement is followed by several suggested answers or completions. Select the one that BEST answers the question or completes the statement. *PRINT THE LETTER OF THE CORRECT ANSWER IN THE SPACE AT THE RIGHT.*

1. In the maxillary periapical radiographs shown at the right, the arrows labeled 1 represent the 1.____

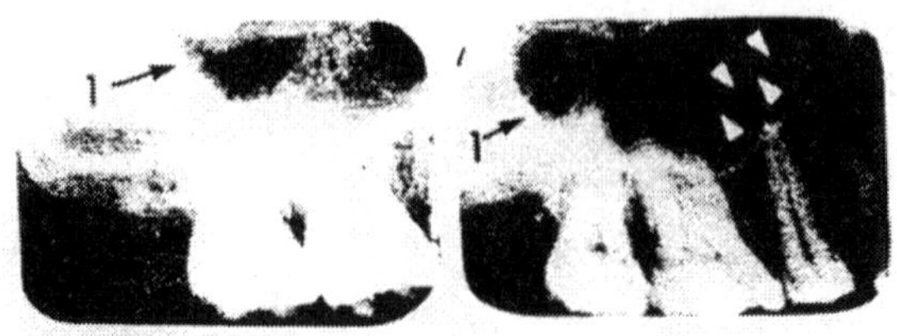

   A. coronoid process
   B. pterygoid hamulus
   C. lateral pterygoid plate
   D. malar process of the maxilla
   E. floor of the nasal cavity

2. In the maxillary periapical radiograph shown at the right, the apex of the small triangle points to the 2.____

   A. retained primary root
   B. posterior nasal spine
   C. floor of the nasal cavity
   D. anterior wall of the maxillary sinus
   E. lateral wall of the maxillary sinus

3. In the maxillary periapical radiograph shown at the right, the circled area is 3.____

   A. the canine fossa
   B. a supernumerary tooth
   C. the floor of the antrum
   D. the anterior nasal spine
   E. a nasolabial palatine duct cyst

4. In the maxillary periapical radiograph shown at the right, number 1 represents the 4.____

   A. maxillary sinus
   B. malar extension
   C. periapical cyst of the maxillary first premolar
   D. periapical abscess of the maxillary first premolar
   E. periapical granuloma of the maxillary first premolar

5. From radiographic evidence alone, the MOST likely interpretation of the area indicated by the arrow in the illustration shown at the right is 5.____

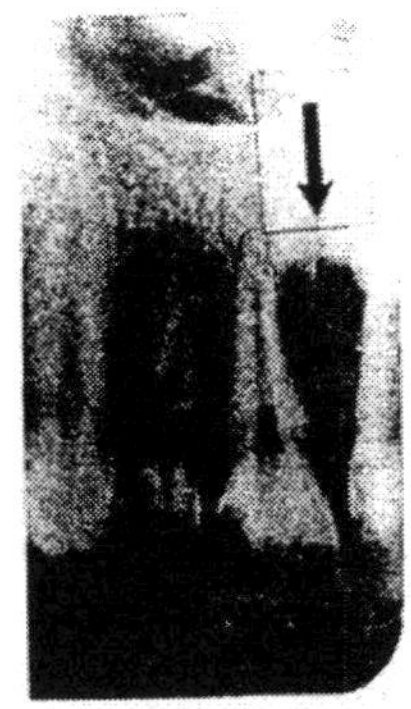

A. a radicular cyst
B. a dental granuloma
C. the incisive fossa
D. a globulomaxillary cyst
E. a chronic periapical abscess

6. In the absence of visual evidence or clinical symptoms, the MOST likely interpretation of the area indicated by the arrow on the radiograph shown at the right would be a 6.____

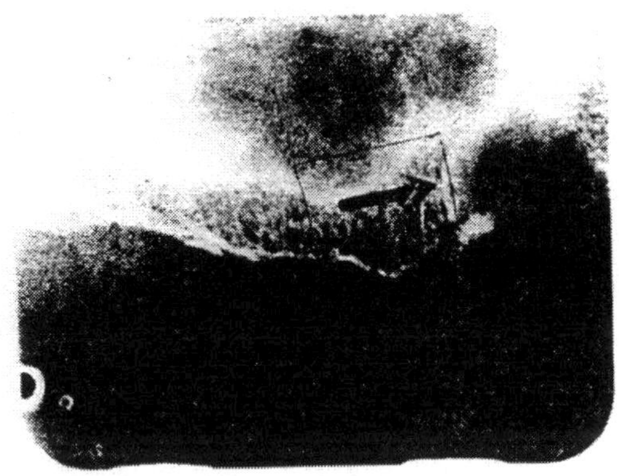

A. residual cyst
B. maxillary sinus
C. surgical defect
D. primordial cyst
E. any of the above

7. The lesion illustrated at the right was excised from the lower lip of a 14-year-old boy. It consists of a central cavity filled with fluid and lined with granulation tissue. A few collections of salivary gland acini were found deep to the lesion. The diagnosis is 7.____

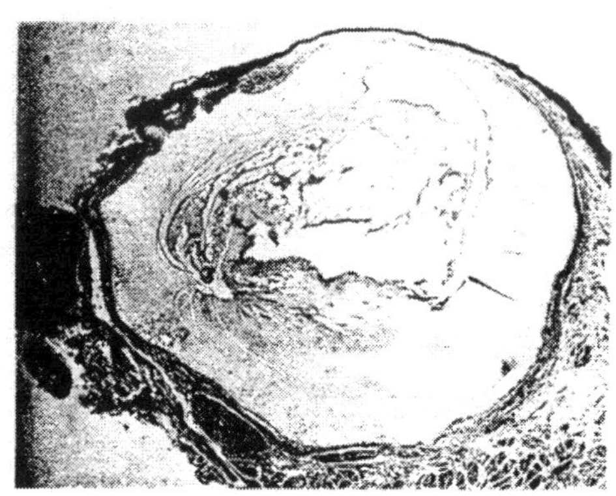

A. ranula
B. fibroma
C. mucocele
D. sebaceous cyst
E. pleomorphic adenoma

8. Refer to the radiograph shown at the right. All teeth are vital. The patient is asymptomatic. How many unerupted supernumerary teeth are present? 8.____

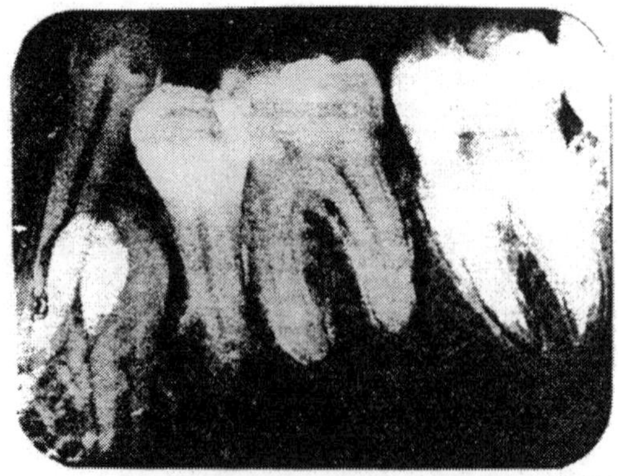

A. 1
B. 2
C. 3
D. 4
E. none of the above

9. The firm, painless lesion of the palate illustrated at the right has been present for at least 10 years and has increased in size very slowly.
The MOST likely diagnosis is 9.____

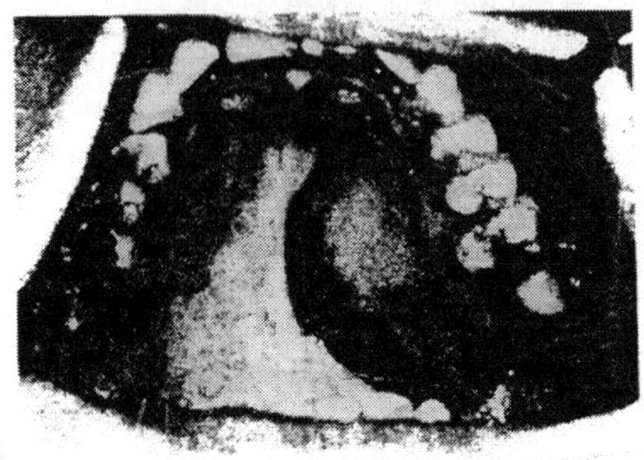

A. torus palatinus
B. retention cyst
C. median palatal cyst
D. pleomorphic adenoma
E. carcinoma of the antrum

10. Condition B indicated in the radiograph shown at the right is MOST likely 10.____

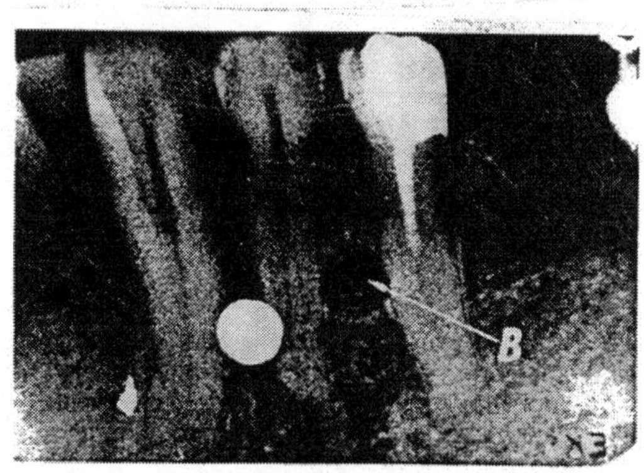

A. an artifact
B. the lingual foramen
C. abnormal cancellous bone
D. a lateral periodontal cyst
E. a salivary gland herniation defect

11. Which of the following is MOST valuable in determining x-ray beam quality? 11.____

A. Homogeneity coefficient
B. Effective photon energy
C. Peak kilovoltage with added filtration
D. Spectral distribution of photon energies
E. Any of the above

12. To determine the anterior-posterior extent of a lesion in the posterior mandibular area, which of the following radiographic projections should be used? 12.____

A. Water view
B. PA of the mandible
C. Distal-oblique
D. Lateral-oblique
E. Mesial-oblique

13. Which of the following salivary gland neoplasms is LEAST likely to be found in the minor glands? 13.____

A. Adenocarcinoma
B. Pleomorphic adenoma
C. Acinic cell carcinoma
D. Mucoepidermoid carcinoma
E. Papillary cystadenoma lymphomatosum

14. Which of the following lesions is LEAST likely to cause root resorption? 14.____

A. Dentigerous cyst
B. Periapical granuloma
C. Globulomaxillary cyst
D. Periapical cemental dysplasia
E. Radicular cyst

15. Which of the following odontogenic tumors exhibits the LEAST inductive influence upon the mesenchymal component of lesional tissues? 15.____

A. Ameloblastoma
B. Compound odontoma
C. Ameloblastic fibroma
D. Ameloblastic fibro-odontoma
E. None of the above

16. Which of the following is NOT a complication of therapeutic radiation to the head and neck? 16.____

A. Mucositis
B. Xerostomia
C. Cervical caries
D. Osteoradionecrosis
E. Paresthesia of the tongue

17. Which of the following will NOT reduce radiation exposure dose per film? 17.____

A. Use of faster film
B. Reduced beam diameter
C. Reduced total filtration
D. Increased development time
E. Increased source-film distance

18. Which of the following conditions is NOT hereditary? 18.____

A. Mottled enamel
B. Amelogenesis imperfecta
C. Cleidocranial dysostosis
D. Dentinogenesis imperfecta
E. Anhidrotic ectodermal dysplasia

19. Which of the following is NOT a clinical manifestation of thrombocytopenia? 19.____

A. Epistaxis
B. Petechiae
C. Ecchymosis
D. Gingival bleeding
E. Gingival hyperplasia

20. Which of the following diseases is NOT associated with loss of the lamina dura? 20.____

A. Osteoporosis
B. Osteomalacia
C. Osteopetrosis
D. Hyperparathyroidism
E. All of the above

KEY (CORRECT ANSWERS)

1. D
2. C
3. D
4. A
5. C

6. A
7. C
8. B
9. D
10. D

11. D
12. C
13. E
14. D
15. A

16. E
17. C
18. A
19. E
20. C

BASIC FUNDAMENTALS OF ORAL PATHOLOGY

CONTENTS

BASIC FUNDAMENTALS OF ORAL PATHOLOGY

Section I. INTRODUCTION

1. General

Pathology is the study of disease, especially in reference to structural and functional changes in tissues and organs which cause or are caused by disease. Oral pathology is that branch of pathology which deals with diseases of the oral cavity. Disease is a particular destructive process in an organism, usually with a specific cause and characteristic symptoms. To describe pathology, oral pathology, and disease, certain terms are used. Local (localized) means the disease is restricted to a part or small area of the body. General (generalized) means the disease affects many or all parts of the body or covers a large area of the body. Incipient refers to a disease or disorder which is just beginning. Severe refers to an intense case of a disease or disorder. Acute refers to a disease or disorder which is severe but of short duration. Chronic refers to a disease or disorder of long duration.

2. Inflammation and Repair (fig. 1)

The capacity of the human body to restore damaged tissues to health varies with the particular type of tissue or cells involved. Wornout cells are replaced and tissues rebuilt as a normal physiologic process to bring about the growth and repair of the body as a whole. When a tissue is injured or irritated by mechanical, chemical, thermal, or bacterial agents it becomes inflamed. Inflammation is the reaction of a tissue to an injurious agent. Clinical inflammation is followed by repair, but repair can occur without clinical inflammation. The body does not always overcome the attack and so disease persists. For example, the irritation produced by dental caries may result in inflammation of the pulp. This pulpal inflammation is called pulpitis. (The suffix "itis" indicates that inflammation exists.) In every case the inflammatory condition results from some form of irritation and to restore normal function to the tissues, the cause must be eliminated.

3. Stages of Inflammation

There are three stages of inflammation: vascular changes, exudation, and resolution and repair. All stages may occur in the same area at the same time. The vascular changes involve hyperemia, in which the blood vessels are dilated and the flow of blood is slower; stasis, in which the flow of blood or body fluid is stopped; changes in the blood and walls of the small vessels; and exudation, which involves the outpouring of fluid substances in or upon the tissues. These changes in the vascular system result in accumulation of fluids in the tissue (edema).

4. Major Signs and Symptoms of Inflammation

The four major signs of inflammation are swelling, pain, heat, and redness. Sometimes a fifth sign is disturbance of function. Swelling is the visual sign of the accumulation of inflammatory substances (exudates) in the tissues and the increased amount of blood in the area. The pressure of the exudates (and perhaps the action of toxins, enzymes, and acids) on the nerve endings causes pain; and the inflammatory involvement of the tissue may result in disturbance of function. The redness and heat which accompany inflammation are due to the increased amount of blood in the area.

5. Beneficial Effects of Inflammation

The beneficial effects of inflammation are essentially fourfold. First, the increased fluid dilutes the irritants present in the area (e.g., bacteria and their poisonous products). Second, the blood cells engulf and often digest bacteria, dead cells, or other debris which might cause or perpetuate the inflammation. Third, antibodies, which are also present in the edema fluid, neutralize toxic substances. Fourth, clotting of the edema fluid walls off the area and prevents the irritant and the inflammation from spreading beyond its effective area.

6. Types of Wound Repair

When the inflammatory process has served its purpose, repair is usually initiated. The cells in the area of injury proliferate, organize into a state much like their old form and, in most cases, resume previous

2

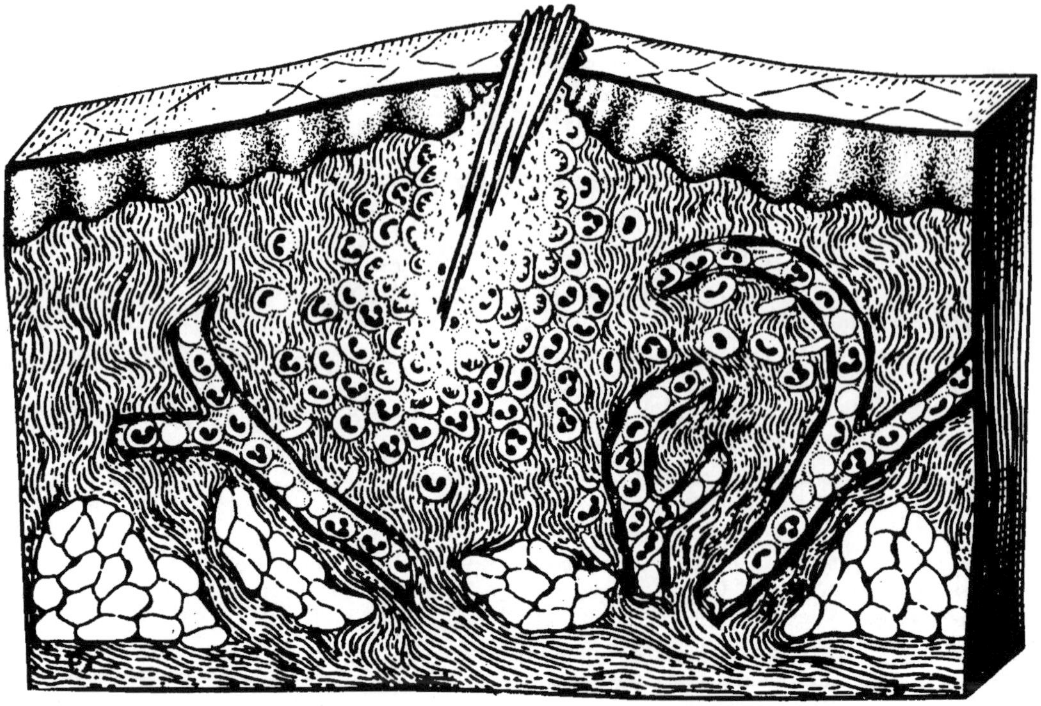

Figure -1. Tissue changes in inflammation.

functions. When the edges of a clean aseptic wound are closely approximated, proliferative connective tissue cells join the walls of the wound and proliferative epithelial cells close over the surface. This type of wound repair is called healing by first intention. If the wound edges are not brought together or are exposed to irritants or infections, granulation tissue forms on the opposing surfaces and fills the space. This granulation tissue containing blood clot, fibroblasts and angioblasts is gradually converted into fibrous tissue, and the old epithelial cells at the wound edges proliferate and cover the surface of the new fibrous tissue.

7. Suppuration

Suppuration is the formation of pus. It often accompanies inflammation. Pus is composed of leukocytes, broken-down cells, serum, bacteria (dead or alive), and inflammatory debris.

8. Abscess

An abscess is a circumscribed area of pus surrounded by a restraining wall of tissue. This most often occurs within the substances of a tissue or organ. A narrow tube or channel which often develops to afford drainage of the abscess is called a fistula or sinus. A periapical abscess is a collection of pus at the apex of the tooth. It is caused by the spread of infection through the apical foramen to the periapical tissues. A periodontal abscess (parietal abscess) is a collection of pus along the sides of the tooth but usually not involving the apical area. It may be caused by a foreign object forced into the periodontal tissues. Abscesses are often clinically manifested by swelling.

9. Ulcer

An ulcer is an open sore other than a wound. The base of an ulcer is composed of granulation tissue resulting from the body's attempt at healing and repair.

10. Cellulitis

If inflammation is not controlled and contained within a localized area, but instead spreads through the substance of the tissue or organ, the condition is called cellulitis. In cellulitis, swelling usually develops rapidly with high fever. The skin usually becomes very red and the area is characterized by severe throbbing pain as the inflammation localizes (fig. 2). The condition is often associated with periapical, periodontal, or pericoronal infections.

Section II. DENTAL CARIES

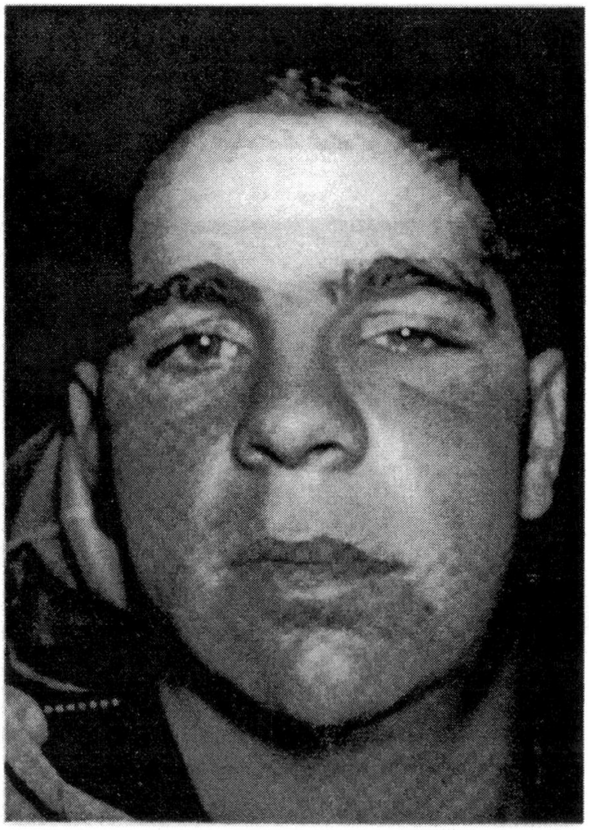

Figure 3–2. Cellulitis of the jaw.

ing the apical portion of the root and the formation of an abscess. The control of dental caries is a very important problem which is receiving much attention in the fields of research and prevention.

11. General

Dental caries is a term for the process commonly referred to as decay of the teeth. Thus, a decayed tooth is properly termed a carious tooth. Dental caries or dental decay is a specific disease which brings about the dissolution and disintegration of the hard structures of the tooth—enamel, cementum and dentin. (The word caries or decay refers to the disease, the word cavity refers to the lesion or hole in the tooth.) Dental caries is the most widespread disease affecting the human race. The incidence of the disease is greatest during childhood and young adulthood. It attacks deciduous teeth the same as it attacks permanent teeth. Dental caries is progressively destructive. It usually begins in a minute area on the enamel or cementum and, if untreated, progresses to the dentin. The next step is penetration to and involvement of the pulp. Infection and death of the pulp may follow with possible extension of the infection into the tissues surrounding the apical portion of the root and the formation of an abscess. The control of dental caries is a very important problem which is receiving much attention in the fields of research and prevention.

12. Causes

In general, dental caries occurs as a result of improper or poor oral hygiene. The destruction of dental tissue by caries, however, is governed somewhat by the susceptibility of the teeth. Little is known about susceptibility or resistance to caries, but the degree of susceptibility may be influenced by certain factors, including diet and oral hygiene, and some systemic diseases. Study of the direct cause of dental caries is very complex; only two theories of its cause are considered here. According to the acidogenic (producing acid) concept, bacteria and their metabolic products accumulate in mucinous plaques, which are often invisible and adhere tightly to the teeth. The bacteria in the plaques produce enzymes that attack carbohydrates and convert them to organic acids. These acids dissolve the enamel and allow deeper bacterial penetration into the tooth. The lesion is progressive. According to the proteolytic (effecting the digestion of proteins) concept, proteolytic bacteria attack the organic material in the enamel (which is mostly protein) along certain tracts called lamellae, which provide passages for the bacteria to enter the dentin. According to both concepts, dental caries is the result of microbial activity on the teeth. The process of dental caries may be a combination of both concepts, with the acidogenic concept accounting for dissolution of mineral content and the proteolytic concept accounting for destruction of organic content of the tooth.

13. Caries in Enamel
(fig. 3)

The organisms that produce acid are contained in mucin plaques which adhere to the surface of the enamel. In improperly cleaned mouths, common sites are pits, fissures, interproximal areas, and along the free margin of the gingivae, particularly on the facial surface of the tooth. The enamel rods of a tooth are cemented together by a substance which dissolves more readily than the rods themselves, and thus, according to the acidogenic concept, the first effect in enamel caries is probably the dissolution of this cementing substance. The first visible evidence of caries is a slightly whitened area on the surface of the tooth, which is very easily overlooked, particularly when the teeth are wet. Drying of the tooth surface makes these areas far more visible. As the acid continues to dissolve the cementing substances, the enamel rods are left without support and break away. Since enamel contains a very small amount of organic material, the formation of a cavity is probably mainly the result of the action of acid, with but limited destruction by putrefaction (enzymic decomposition, especially of proteins).

14. Caries in Dentin
(fig. 3)

From the small area on the surface of the tooth, caries continues its progressive destruction, first penetrating the dentinoenamel junction, and then spreading laterally and directly within the dentin

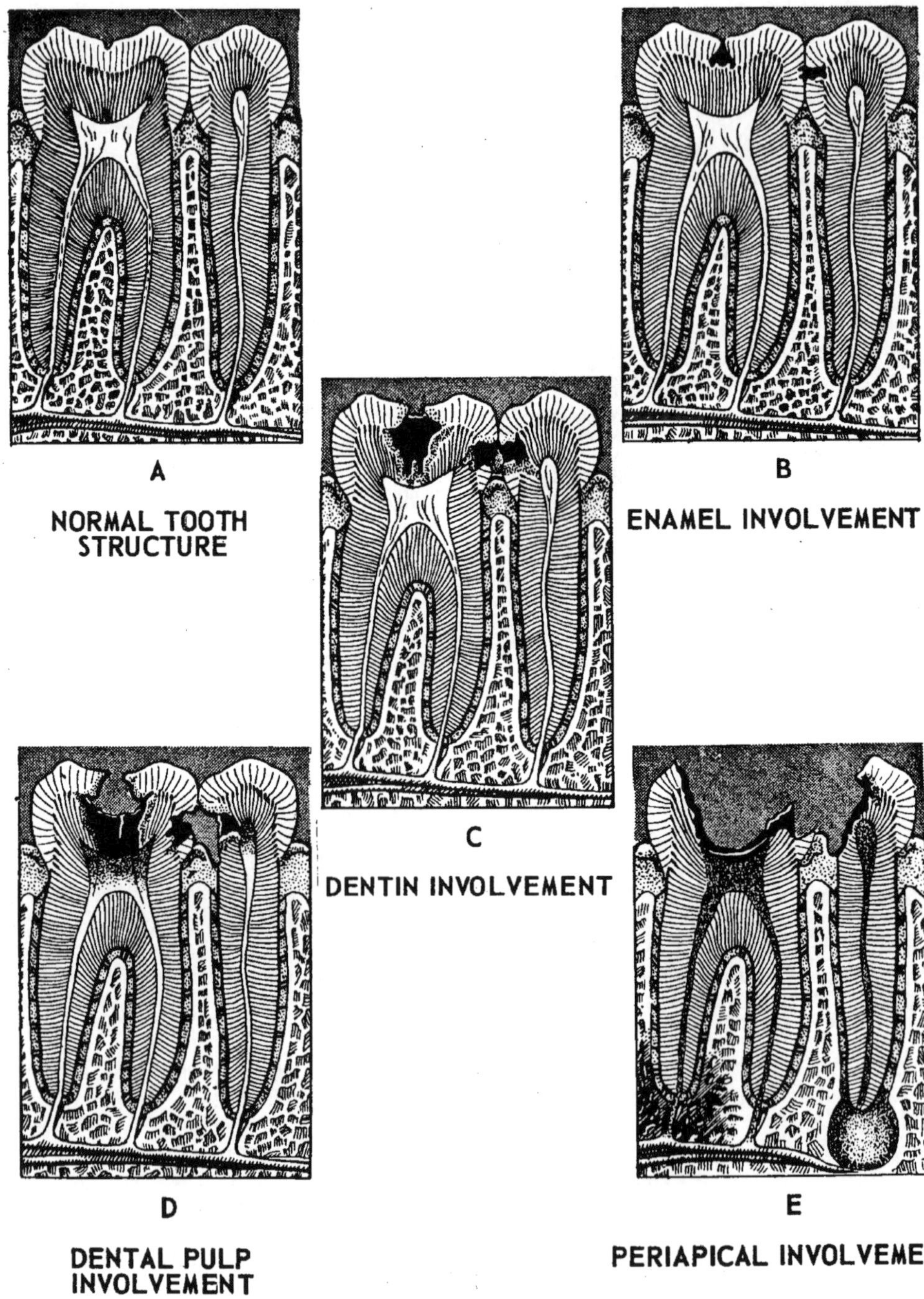

Figure 3. Stages in the progress of dental caries.

toward the pulp. Thus, what may appear to the patient as a small surface cavity may, in reality, be a very extensive involvement of the tooth structure.

a. The destructive process of caries differs in dentin and enamel. In caries of enamel, the organisms cannot enter the substance of the enamel until the acid produced by the organisms has destroyed the enamel substance. The reverse is true of the dentin, which is made up of many hollow tubules. Because these tubules offer a natural pathway for penetration by bacteria and because the dentin contains a large proportion of organic materials, progression is faster in dentin than in enamel. When dentin has been reached, acid-forming and proteolytic organisms can enter the dentinal tubules and produce acid or break down the organic matrix within the tissue itself. Since dentinal tubules tend to branch and communicate with each other at the dentinoenamel junction, the organisms penetrate the dentin laterally in all directions along this junction. Accompanying this lateral penetration is a penetration along the main tubules in the direction of the pulp. This lateral and direct involvement tends to form a cone-shaped area of decay, with the apex of the cone pointed toward the pulp of the tooth and the base at the dentinoenamel junction.

b. Although dentin destruction in caries is normally faster than enamel destruction, the rapidity of dentin destruction both in depth and breadth will be governed by its structure. Because of the extensive organic matrix of the dentin, enough substance is left after the dissolution of the inorganic salts to retain its physical form until further destruction has taken place by the process of putrefaction.

c. Caries in the dentin is described as having an infected layer and an affected layer. In the infected dentin many micro-organisms are present and most of the dentinal tubules have been destroyed through demineralization and putrefaction. This layer is soft on the surface but gets tough, leathery, or rubbery underneath. Below the infected dentin, the affected dentin is found. Few micro-organisms are found in this area and the dentinal tubules are intact. Depending on the extent of the lesion, normal dentin is found under affected dentin. The difference in these layers plays an important role in the treatment of caries in the dentin.

15. Arrested Caries

Arrested caries is the stage where the progress of the decay process has stopped. The softened dentin has been lost or worn away so that the discolored (either yellow, brown, or black), sound, hard dentin remains and has a polished look.

16. Pulpal Reaction to Dental Caries (fig. 3)

a. Dental pulp, which is located in the pulp chamber and root canals of teeth, is a highly vascular tissue. The blood supply comes to it and leaves it by way of blood vessels entering and leaving the narrow apical foramen or foramina. When pulp tissue is diseased, the exudation accompanying inflammation has nowhere to go but through these apical openings and, since they are already occupied by blood vessels and nerves, pressure builds up inside the chamber. This pressure causes pain and constricts the blood vessels. In addition, the nerves are pinched between the tooth structure and the swelling, thus producing severe pain.

b. The reaction of the pulp to dental caries varies. Often this variation is in accordance with the rate of advance of the carious process. Before there is much dentin involvement, the pulp tissue becomes irritated and the irritation causes inflammation and swelling. This, in turn, stimulates the odontoblasts to produce secondary dentin in an effort to protect the pulp. If the rate of advance of caries is slow and the resistance of the patient is high, this deposition of secondary dentin may prevent the carious process from reaching the pulp tissues for a considerable time. If it were not for this protective reaction of the odontoblasts, a far higher percentage of carious lesions would reach the pulp chamber before detection, with exposure and death of the pulp. If not treated or arrested, the carious process eventually reaches and involves the pulp tissue. As it nears the pulp, the irritation becomes more severe and bacterial invasion occurs, followed by an inflammatory process. The swelling of tissue usually accompanies inflammation. If the inflammation is severe or of prolonged duration, the pulp tissue presses against the hard, unyielding walls of the pulp chamber and root canals. As a result of this pressure and the reduction of blood supply caused by constriction of blood vessels, the involved pulp tissue dies.

Section III. DISEASES OF THE DENTAL PULP

17. General

Dental pulp is a sensitive tissue subject to many irritations resulting from dental caries, exposure to excessive heat or cold, and mechanical, chemical, or electrical stimulation. In a healthy tooth the enamel and periodontal tissues act as mechanical and insulating coverings. If the enamel or cemental tissues covering the root are damaged or removed, exposing the underlying dentin, the dentin becomes sensitive to external irritants because the Tomes' fibers transmit sensations to the nerve tissue in the pulp. The initial response to irritation is an increase of blood in the small arteries (arterioles) of the pulp (active hyperemia). These changes cause pressure on the nerve fibers in the pulp, often severe enough to produce pain. Hyperemia is usually temporary and, since it is reversible, the pulp will return to normal if the irritation is removed. If it remains, progressively destructive changes will take place. Among the diseases which affect the pulp are acute pulpitis, chronic pulpitis, pulp abscesses, hyperplastic pulpitis, and a number of degenerative changes. Acute and chronic pulpitis and pulp abscesses are commonly encountered in clinical dental practice.

18. Acute Pulpitis

Acute inflammatory changes in the pulp are often caused by organisms which have gained access to the exposed pulp. These changes may be an early response to pulpal infection or a flareup of a chronic inflammation. The active growth of the organisms in the environment of the pulp produces rapid destructive changes. These are accompanied by symptoms which are correspondingly severe. Clinically, severe pulsating pain is caused by the rapid buildup of pressure. Application of cold to the tooth gives some relief; release of pressure by opening into the pulp chamber or by spontaneous release following a break of infection through periapical tissues brings almost immediate relief. If the condition is severe enough it may be accompanied by fever, headache, and malaise. As the inflammation progresses, it gradually involves the entire pulp, spreading to the periapical tissues and causing the tooth to become loosened and sensitive to externally applied pressure. It may pass beyond the periapical tissues to involve the surrounding bone and perforate the periosteum and overlying tissues to drain either into the mouth or through the skin extraorally.

19. Chronic Pulpitis

Chronic pulpitis is often accompanied by bacterial infection. It may be the result of persistent mild to moderate irritation of the pulp, or may follow a period of acute pulpitis. Chronic infection of the pulp may recover, continue with slow destruction of the entire pulp and involvement of the periapical tissues, or develop into an acute infection in the presence of virulent organisms which have reached the pulp from the mouth. Chronic pulpitis may be accompanied by no pain or by intermittent periods of mild to moderate pain associated with periods of increased activity and buildup of pressure in the pulp chamber and root canals.

20. Pulp Abscess

Localized areas of infection (abscesses) may develop within the crown portion of the pulp tissue. They may be found in teeth in which restorations have been placed or in teeth having no detectable defect. They produce a severe, intermittent pain which is increased when the patient lies down and which usually responds to application of cold with a sharp pain tapering off to a dull pulsation. It is often difficult to identify the affected tooth because of the absence of caries or other identifiable cause and because there is no involvement of the periapical tissues, so that the tooth does not differ from the other teeth in its sensitivity to percussion or other externally applied pressure.

21. Hyperplastic Pulpitis

Hyperplastic pulpitis is occasionally encountered in deciduous teeth as an enlargement of the pulp, representing an unusually excessive reaction to inflammation. In this condition, the pulp tissue extrudes through a perforation in the pulp chamber and is seen as a soft palpable mass exposed in the crown portion of the tooth.

22. Degenerative Changes of the Pulp

Since the pulp of the tooth is subjected to a variety of bacterial, mechanical, or chemical irritations, degenerative changes often occur within the pulp. Types of degenerative changes include hyaline degeneration, calcific degeneration, pulp stones, and fibrosis. Degenerative changes seldom have any clinical significance; to a certain extent, they are normal physiological processes.

Section IV. DISEASES OF THE PERIAPICAL TISSUE

23. General

In all conditions which cause death of the pulp, infection probably will pass through the apical foramina into the adjacent tissues. Among the resulting diseases are acute periapical inflammation, dental granuloma, radicular cyst, and acute periapical abscess. Extensions of infections originating in teeth may lead to such diseases as osteomyelitis and Ludwig's angina.

24. Acute Periapical Inflammation

Acute inflammation of the periapical tissue usually represents an extension of acute pulpal inflammation. This area may be invaded by nonpyogenic bacteria, which results in a transposition to a chronic inflammation.

25. Dental Granuloma

Chronic inflammation of periapical tissues may follow acute inflammation of the same tissues or may be the direct result of the effects of a nonvital, infected pulp. Inflammatory processes usually take place very slowly. With time there is a destruction of bone in the immediate surrounding area and a fibrous capsule may form around the area of infection. The fibers of this capsule blend with those of the periodontal ligament, often causing the capsule and inclosed material to adhere to the tooth when it is extracted. Dental granulomas are so named because they are made up of granulomatous tissue. Dental granulomas may remain chronically active without symptoms for years, or they may flare up following invasion of organisms. Increased activity and pressure may cause a breakthrough to the oral mucosa resulting in formation of a sinus (fistulous) tract or channel through which the products of the infection drain, or may lead to other complications associated with acute infection. The continued presence of an area of chronic infection such as a dental granuloma constitutes a potential focus of infection for other areas of the body.

26. Radicular Cyst

A radicular cyst is a cyst associated with the root of a tooth. It begins as an inflammatory process and develops very much as does a dental granuloma. The major difference between a dental granuloma and a radicular cyst is that the capsule of the granuloma is made up of connective tissue fibers, while that of the cyst is lined with epithelium. The source of the epithelium is probably the remnants of the epithelial sheath which influenced the formation of root dentin during the development of the tooth. Granulomas normally will disappear through repair following removal of the cause. Cysts, if not removed, may increase in size. A cyst may get so big that it involves a large portion of the jaw in which it is located. Cysts may be relatively inactive and painless, or they may cause pain or tenderness.

27. Acute Periapical Abscess

An acute periapical abscess is nearly always the result of an exacerbation of an existing chronic infection which extends from an infected pulp or is present as a dental granuloma. Although these abscesses take various clinical forms, they are characterized by the formation of pus and extension of the infective process due to increased activity and pressure within the infected area. The involved tooth usually becomes increasingly painful to touch. In some cases the abscess, if allowed to continue, makes its way through the bone and overlying tissues to open and drain into the mouth or on the face; the dental officer may facilitate final penetration of soft tissue by incision of the area. Once the tissues have been perforated and pressure lessened, there is almost dramatic relief of pain.

28. Osteomyelitis

Osteomyelitis is an inflammation of the bone marrow which, when located in the jaws, may be caused by infected teeth, other infections of the jaws, or trauma. Fortunately, osteomyelitis of the jaw is relatively uncommon in comparison to the high incidence of infected teeth. Osteomyelitis can be a serious infection, difficult to control. Antibiotic drugs have greatly improved treatment of this disease.

29. Ludwig's Angina

Acute infections which invade the floor of the mouth may spread into the tissues of the neck causing a cellulitis characterized by a hard, boardlike swelling of those tissues. The condition is known as Ludwig's angina, a relatively rare but dangerous infection. It is commonly accompanied by high temperature, pain, and serious interference with breathing. Fatality may occur from suffocation or exhaustion. Extensions of infection from carious teeth, the salivary glands, or the tonsils may cause this disease.

Section V. EROSION, ABRASION, AND RESORPTION

30. General

There are four types of conditions besides dental caries in which there is loss of tooth substance—erosion, abrasion, resorption, and total or partial avulsion. Erosion is the chemical wearing away of the tooth structure. In abrasion, which can be seen clinically, the cause is the mechanical wearing away of the tooth substance. Resorption, which can be seen on a radiograph and which involves the loss of tooth structure, is not clearly understood. Avulsion is the loss of the tooth due to trauma.

31. Erosion

(fig. 4)

Erosion is usually found on the external surface at the neck of the tooth. It appears as various shapes cut into the surface at the neck of the tooth. Under these areas there is a calcification of dentinal tubules and irregularly deposited dentin. The enamel and dentin are usually hard and shiny. In certain cases the crowns may be almost severed from the roots.

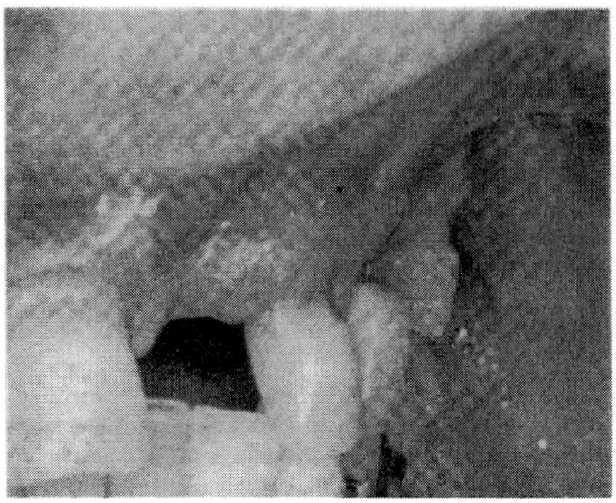

Figure 4. Erosion.

32. Abrasion and Attrition

In abrasion, one or more teeth may show the effects of wear. The wearing of the tooth substance may be caused by biting some foreign substance such as a pipe stem or a bobby pin, by faulty toothbrushing techniques, or by nervous biting habits. Abrasion and attrition (fig. 5) differ in that attrition is considered a normal gradual loss of tooth substance from the chewing of food and it involves all the teeth with the cusps and contact points of all teeth showing uniform wear. If the loss of tooth substance is excessive, it is called abrasion. In either case, the dentinal tubules may become calcified and secondary or irregular dentin may be deposited in the pulp immediately below them. Secondary cementum may be laid down about the roots.

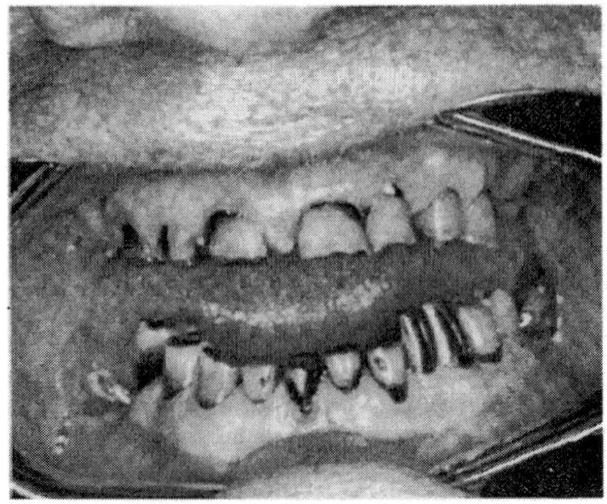

Figure 5. Abrasion.

33. Resorption

In resorption, there is dissolution of tissues by body fluids or cellular activity. Osteoclasts and cementoclasts are the cells which are active in the resorption of bone and cementum. The condition is evident most often in the alveolar process and in the roots of teeth. Certain types of resorption may be considered normal, and other types may be the result of abnormal conditions.

a. The roots of temporary teeth normally are resorbed just before the eruption of the permanent teeth. There is also normal resorption of bone in elderly individuals and in edentulous areas where permanent teeth have been extracted. Healthy bone is constantly being rebuilt. Resorption and deposition of bone is the basis for the treatment applied by the orthodontist who moves malposed teeth slowly into proper occlusion. Resorption is also important in the repair of fractures and the healing of tooth sockets.

b. Other types of resorption may not be considered normal. Resorption in the roots of permanent teeth may be the result of many factors involving disease and trauma. Systemic (endocrine) disturbances and some neoplasms, for example, are characterized by bone and root resorption; and impacted teeth may impinge upon the roots of other teeth to cause areas of resorption.

Section VI. PERIODONTAL DISEASES

34. General

Periodontal diseases are diseases which involve the periodontal tissues. A consideration of the causes of these diseases involves both systemic and local factors.

35. Gingivitis
(figs. 6 and 7)

Gingivitis is an inflammation of the gingival tissues. It is characterized by the typical signs and symptoms of inflammation—swelling, redness, pain, increased heat, and, sometimes, disturbance of function. In normal gingival tissue minimal inflammatory activity is always present. It is felt that this inflammation is caused by the toxic substances produced by bacteria in the mucin plaques adjacent to the gingival tissue. Direct irritation from food impaction, toothbrush bristles, or toothpicks also can cause gingival inflammation. With inflammation the gingival tissue appears to grow and the gingival sulcus around the tooth is deepened, allowing debris to accumulate and more plaque to form. If these plaques are not removed, they may become calcified from the precipitation of calcium salts from the saliva. The calcified plaque is called calculus.

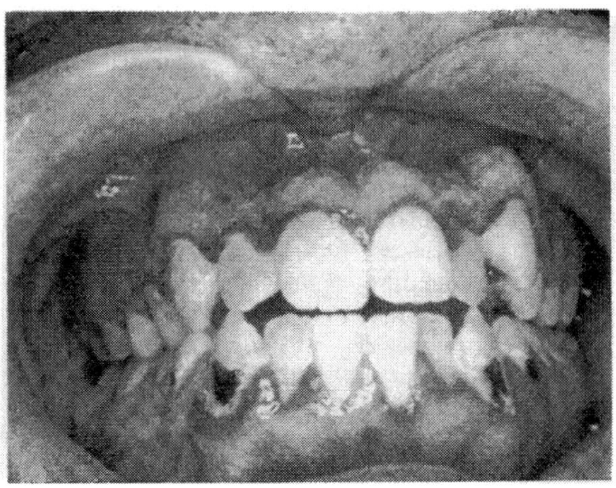

Figure 6. Marginal gingivitis.

36. Vincent's Infection (Necrotizing Ulcerative Stomatitis)

Vincent's infection, commonly called "trench mouth," is a bacterial infection. It is usually associated with poor oral hygiene but is occasionally seen in the presence of good oral hygiene.

a. Although the exact cause of the disease is unknown, two organisms—the fusiform bacillus and Vincent's spirillum—are considered the exciting causes of the disease. It is doubtful that Vincent's infection is communicable. Instruction in oral and personal hygiene is not only an important preventive measure but also an essential phase of the treatment. The infecting organisms can successfully invade and grow only in tissues whose resistance has

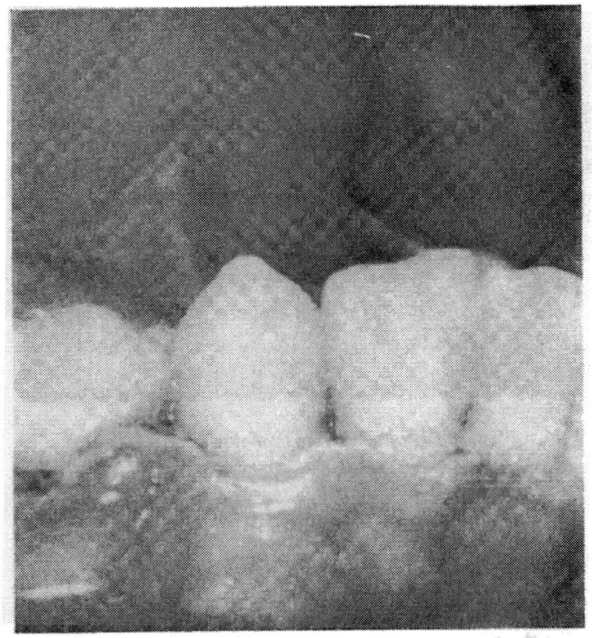

Figure 7. Necrotizing gingivitis.

been lowered. Therefore, proper diet, rest, and exercise can be preventive measures.

b. Vincent's disease is characterized by fetid breath and the appearance of grayish or yellowish-gray ulcers. They may be found in only a few areas or throughout the mouth. The most common site of these ulcers is the marginal or interproximal gingivae or both. The thin gray membrane covering the ulcer may be wiped off easily, exposing a highly inflamed area which bleeds very easily. There is a rather rapid destruction of the marginal and interproximal soft tissue, and these tissues become so painful that it becomes difficult to brush the teeth and to masticate food. The onset of this infection is sudden, and in severe cases there may be a rise in temperature, an increased pulse rate, pallor of the skin, insomnia, and mental depression. Treatment includes procedures performed by the dental officer and home-care procedures performed by the patient.

37. Periodontitis
(figs. 8 and 9)

Periodontitis is an inflammation of the tissues supporting the teeth and the marginal gingivae. It is also known as "pyorrhea alveolaris," "Riggs' disease," or "periodontoclasia." If untreated, the tooth may be lost through destruction of the supporting tissues.

a. Periodontitis is most often caused by deposits of calculus. It is also caused by irritation from poorly fitting crowns, bands, and restorations, and

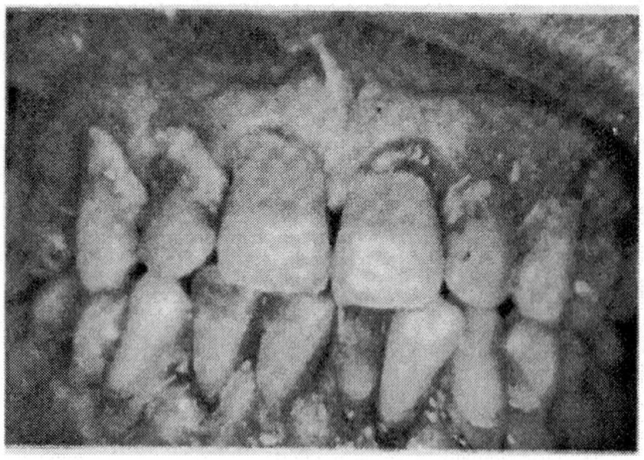

Figure 8. Periodontitis.

impactions of food in crevices. Poor diet, endocrine disturbance, and systemic disease may serve as predisposing factors.

b. In this disease, the periodontal ligament separates from the cementum and a pocket forms between the tooth and the gingival tissue. The pocket becomes an entrance for bacteria. Inflammation follows. Alveolar bone is resorbed and the space created is partly filled with granulation tissue. With loss of bony support, the teeth may become loose. In periodontitis, the gingival tissue may take on a bluish appearance. Bad taste, bleeding gums, and hypersensitive teeth are common symptoms. Treatment includes management of the disease by the dental officer and vigorous home care by the patient.

38. Periodontosis

This is a noninflammatory degenerative disease of the tissues supporting the teeth. In the early stages, the gingival tissue appears normal in color and the teeth are loose without any signs of inflammation. The gingivae separate from the necks of the teeth, and epithelium grows over the pockets that are formed between the teeth and the gingivae. Radiographic examination reveals wide destruction of alveolar bone. As the disease progresses, there are clinical signs of periodontitis. This disease does not respond well to normal forms of treatment and the prognosis is poor.

39. Pericoronitis

(fig. 10)

Periocoronitis is an inflammatory process occurring in gingival "flaps" of tissue found over partially erupted teeth. The most frequent site is the mandibular third or second molar region. The heavy flap of gingival tissues covering portions of the crown of the tooth makes an ideal pocket for debris accumulation and bacterial incubation. In the acute phase, pain and swelling in the area are prominent features. Symptoms of a sore throat and difficulty in swallowing may be present. A partial contraction of muscles of mastication, called trismus, may be experienced. Abscess formation in the area may occur, leading to marked systemic symptoms of general malaise and rise in temperature. Treatment should be directed toward careful cleansing of the pocket area and followup care with hot saline irrigations. Antibiotic therapy may be indicated if the condition

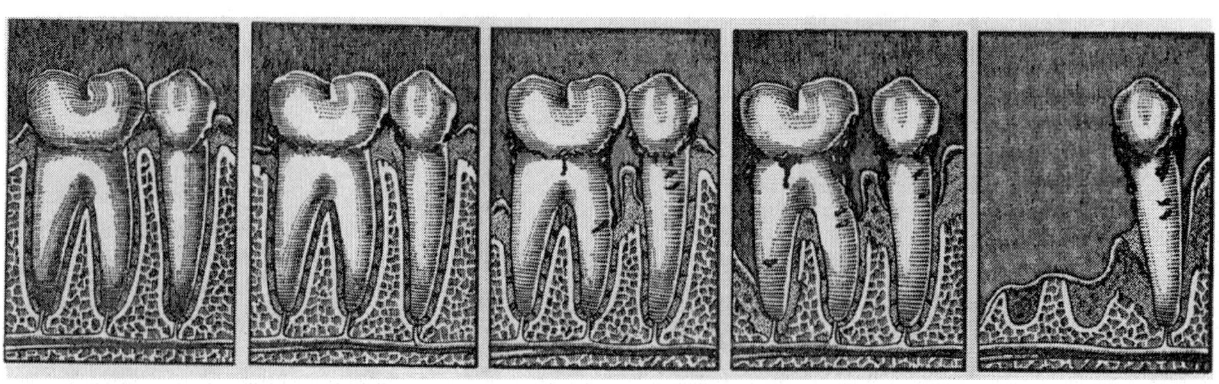

A B C D E

Figure 9. The progress of periodontal destruction.

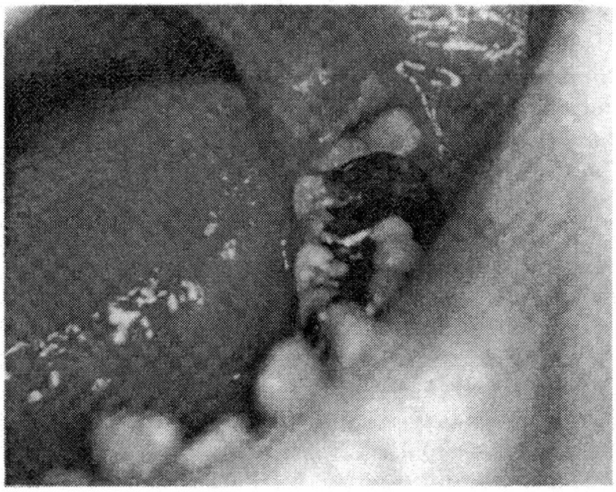

Figure 10. Pericoronitis.

warrants. The prognosis for retention of the tooth is dependent upon the possibility of complete elimination of the inflammation and elimination of the flap.

40. Periodontal Abscess

A periodontal abscess (parietal abscess) is most frequently a sequel of untreated periodontal disease. It is an abscess formation along the side of the tooth. It can be caused by a foreign body, such as calculus, toothpick, or toothbrush bristle, becoming lodged in the periodontal ligament or beneath the free margin of the gingival tissue. A periodontal abscess may drain either through periodontal pockets or through the gingivae into the mouth. The most common signs and symptoms are dull pain in adjacent periodontal tissues, soreness of the gingiva, and shiny mucous membrane over the area.

Section VII. DISEASES OF ORAL MUCOSA

41. Recurrent Herpes Labialis

Herpes simplex (cold sore blisters) is caused by the herpes simplex virus and is often associated with colds, gastrointestinal disturbances, fatigue, fevers, and prolonged exposure to the wind. The common site of occurrence is on the lips (fig. 11) at the junction of the mucous membrane and the skin of the face; however, cold sores may appear on the skin of the face or on the mucous membrane of the cheek, palate, or tongue. The lesions usually consist of clusters of small vesicles which in the early stages contain a clear, transparent fluid. After a few days the vesicles tend to dry up and form a definite crust or scab. The disease is self-limiting and usually disappears in 7 to 10 days.

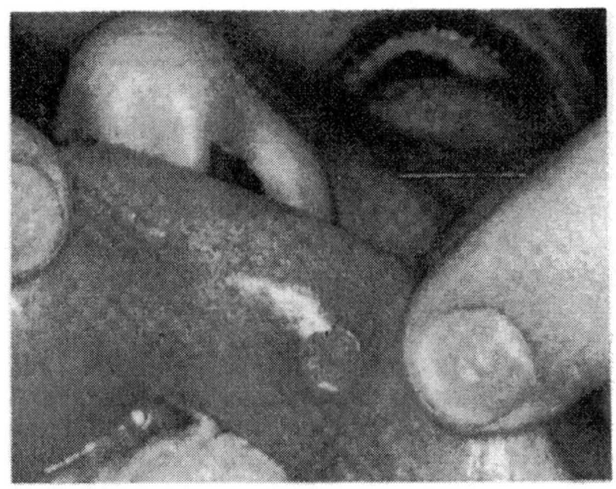

Figure 5-12. Alphthous ulcer on labial mucosa.

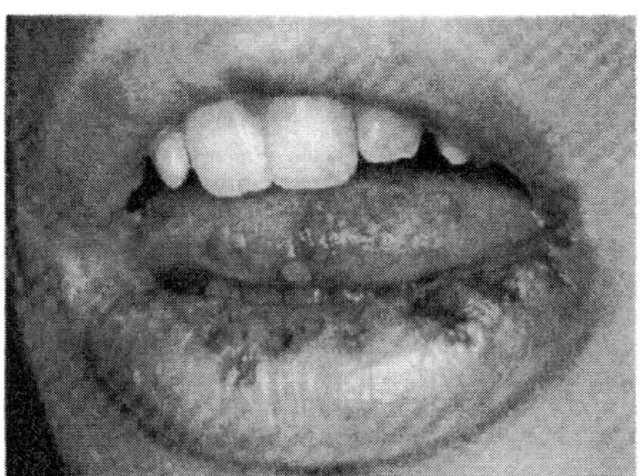

Figure 11. Herpes labialis.

42. Recurrent Aphthous Ulcers

The term "stomatitis" refers to any inflammation of the mucous membrane of the mouth. Aphthous refers to the vesicles which undergo ulceration. This disease may be a more complex form of herpes simplex, however, recent investigations seem to indicate that the aphthous lesion is caused by the transitional L-form of the alpha hemolytic streptococcus. The disease often occurs as multiple lesions in the mouth while herpes simplex is nearly always a single lesion. In the course of this disease, ulcers (fig. 5-12) appear as depressions on the mucous membrane, and are covered by a grayish-white or light yellow membrane. Each ulcer is preceded by a vesicle which normally persists only a few hours before rupturing and producing the ulcer. The ulcers vary in size from a small pinhead to a diameter of ¼ or ½ inch. They may occur in various parts of the mouth, but are most common on the gingival tissue in the region of the mucofacial fold and on the tongue. They are very painful, especially to the touch; this fact, with the appearance of the ulcers, makes diagnosis relatively easy.

43. Syphilis

Syphilis is a venereal disease caused by the organism Treponema pallidum.

a. Primary Syphilis. The first stage of syphilis is characterized by the appearance of the lesion called the chancre. The chancre may appear anywhere on the body but the common site is on the genitalia. It may appear in the oral cavity, where it is characterized by an ulcer with a hard, rolled border. Because it is usually painless, the patient is sometimes unaware of its existence. It normally is a single lesion, although rare cases of two lesions or more are on record. Any hard lesion appearing on the lips or in the mouth should be viewed with suspicion and information secured by laboratory procedures. The chancre is highly infectious and, although it is commonly found on the genitalia, its appearance in the mouth is not rare and the dentist and his assistants, particularly the hygienist, should never overlook the possibility of its presence and the attendant danger of infection to the operator.

b. Secondary Lesions. The secondary stage of syphilis appears from 3 to 8 weeks after the appearance of the primary lesion. It is the result of a generalized involvement of the circulation. Bacteria enter the bloodstream at the site of the primary lesion, multiply, and are carried throughout the body by the circulatory system. Consequently, the secondary lesions may appear anywhere on the body and in large numbers. The lesions which appear on mucous membranes are known as mucous patches. These are probably the most contagious of all syphilitic lesions and are often present on the oral mucosa during the second stage of syphilis. The true mucous patch is usually oval in shape with a moist, glistening, grayish-white, slightly raised surface. Other secondary lesions, however, may have a radically different appearance. That is what makes the clinical diagnosis of secondary syphilis difficult. As in the single primary lesion, the dental officer and his assistants must be suspicious of any lesions of the mucous membrane of the mouth and throat and obtain a correct laboratory diagnosis.

c. Tertiary Syphilis. The third and terminal stage of syphilis may appear at any time from several months to several years after the initial infection. Usually, there are no multiple lesions and often there is just one. The lesions of this stage are not considered very contagious, since they rarely contain the causative organisms. They appear in the mouth but with less frequency than secondary lesions. They normally appear as nodules and slowly get bigger, becoming softer and less dense. Eventually the center of the nodule becomes eroded and a definite ulcer results. The soft tissue and underlying bone are destroyed. Perforations of the soft palate often result.

d. Congenital Syphilis. A mother having syphilis during pregnancy may transmit the disease to the child. Certain tooth formations are considered typical of congenital syphilis. In these cases the central incisors are notched on their incisal edges and are pegshaped, and the cusps of the first molars are underdeveloped. The typically notched, peg-shaped incisors are called Hutchinson's teeth (fig. 13). Deformed (mulberry) molars are another diagnostic sign. The presence of these teeth alone, however, should not be considered sufficient reason for making a diagnosis of congenital syphilis.

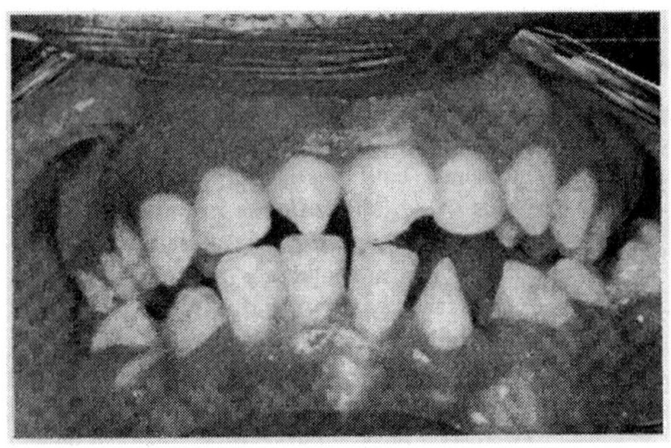

Figure 13. Hutchinson's incisors.

44. Leukoplakia

Leukoplakia is a phenomenon affecting the mucosa, especially of the oral cavity. It is commonly characterized by an irregular thickening of the outer layers of the mucosa, a dull white to gray color, variable size, and very little pain unless ulceration and secondary infection have developed. The cause is unknown but presence of the disease is commonly associated with chronic irritation or trauma, such as might result from smoking, cheek biting, and ill-fitting dentures. The condition very often precedes development of a malignant tumor. For that reason, early diagnosis and treatment are important.

Leukoplakia resembles other conditions which may affect the oral mucous membrane; hence, diagnosis must be based upon microscopic examination of cellular changes within the involved tissues. Tissue specimens are prepared for such examination by a procedure known as "biopsy," (para 84). Once a definitive diagnosis has been made, the treatment of choice is removal of the lesion.

45. Mucosal Injury from Trauma

The most common cause of injury in the oral cavity is trauma. The result may be a thickening of the mucosa with a white appearance, or there may be an ulceration. These lesions are found in an area of the mucosa exposed to injury by the teeth such as chewing the cheek or lip; by food which is excessively hot or spicy; by foreign objects such as a fish bone or toothpick; or by chemicals such as aspirin tablets (fig. 14) held against mucous membrane to relieve toothache. Depending on the cause of trauma, the treatment is usually palliative and the prevention of secondary infection is considered.

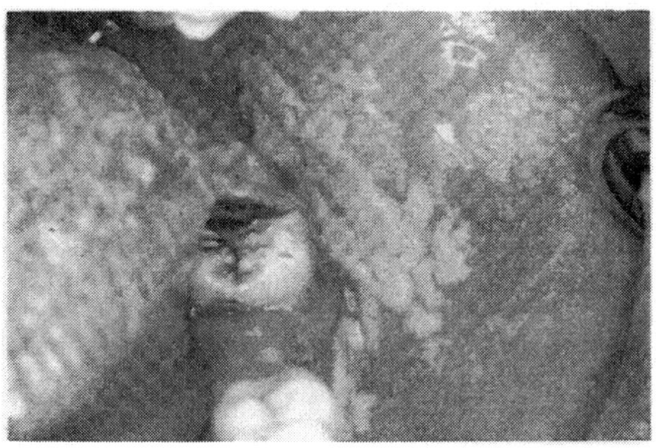

Figure 14. Aspirin burn.

46. Fordyce's Spots.

This condition is due to the presence of sebaceous glands in the mucosa of the lip, cheek, and palate. They are generally seen in the buccal mucosa in the retromolar area. There is no abnormality of the thin epithelial covering. No inflammation is present. The lesion appears as a small, isolated or clustered round elevations (maculopapules) with the color of chamois skin. The lesion is not harmful and generally no treatment is indicated.

47. Stomatitis Nicotina

The act of smoking tobacco causes this disease. The irritating factors of smoking are heat, smoke, and combustion products. These factors affect the palatal glands and produce a stomatitis which may progress to leukoplakia or cancer. Smoking may affect areas other than the palate. The palatal lesions begin as small, round "heaped-up" areas of excess keratin around the openings of the palatal ducts. These openings are obvious when air is blown over them. These lesions may coalesce to form the generalized whitish keratosis. A subjective burning sensation may be present. Treatment requires elimination of the smoking habit. Lesions disappear if degree of keratosis is mild; if severe, a biopsy may be indicated to rule out leukoplakia or cancer.

48. Cheilosis

Cheilosis (fig. 15) usually begins as redness and peeling of the skin at the angles of the mouth. As the condition continues, cracks occur in the skin and mucous membranes at the commissure of the lips. These lesions are often subject to secondary infection and associated with prolonged nutritional deficiencies, especially vitamin A. A condition similar to cheilosis may also be present in patients in whom there has been a noticeable reduction in the vertical dimension because of inadequate dentures or marked abrasion of the natural teeth.

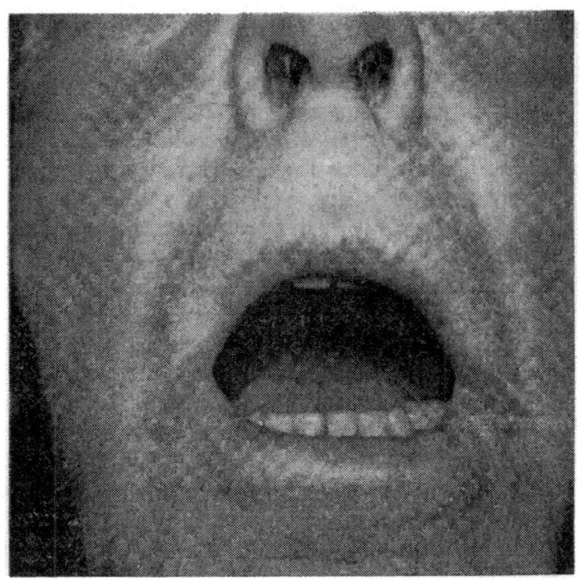

Figure 15. Cheilosis.

49. Denture Irritation

Localized areas of inflammation associated with prostheses can result from a number of factors, which may include occlusal disharmonies, damage to the denture base or metal framework as a result of careless handling, or certain tissue changes. The mucous membrane beneath the denture becomes inflamed and if it is not remedied this chronic irritation may result in hyperplasia of the oral mucosa. Hyperplasia caused by irritation at the border of the denture takes the form of long folds of excess tissue along the denture border. These folds are called epulis fissuratum. Irritation of the palate may result in the development of numerous papillae, a condition called papillary hyperplasia. These two conditions continuing over a long time may result in malignancy.

50. Moniliasis

Moniliasis of the oral mucous membranes, also called thrush, is a surface infection resulting from a yeast-like fungus, Candia albicans. Moniliasis has been recognized in newborn infants, debilitated patients, and patients receiving certain antibiotics. The lesion appears as deposits of white, curdled milk which leave a raw, red, painful surface when scraped off.

51. Allergic Manifestations

a. The allergic condition called angioneurotic edema may be related to food allergy, hypersensitivity, local or focal infection, and endocrine or emotional disturbances. The characteristic symptom is rapid swelling of the affected tissue in 5 to 30 minutes with itching and burning which may persist for 24 hours to days. Areas most commonly involved are the skin about the eyes and chin, the lips, and the tongue. Treatment is symptomatic.

b. Ingestion of certain drugs by individuals having an idiosyncrasy or intolerance to them may result in the allergic manifestations referred to as stomatitis medicamentosa. The signs in the mouth vary from a sensitive erythema to an ulcerative stomatitis or gingivitis. If withdrawal of the suspected drug is followed by disappearance of the lesions, it is evidence of its causal relationships. Therefore, treatment consists of identification and elimination of the drug causing the lesions.

c. While the lesions of stomatitis medicamentosa are the result of absorption of drugs, the lesions of stomatitis venenata are due to the direct contact with a drug or a material. Causative agents of stomatitis veneata may be topical medications, dentifrices, mouthwashes, or denture bases. Intraoral signs may vary from a sensitive erythema to an ulceration. Treatment consists of elimination of the causative agent, local symptomatic care, or use of a mild antibacterial agent to minimize secondary infection of an ulceration.

52. Oral Tori

In about one-fifth of the population, bony outgrowths called tori occur in the midline of the palate or on the lingual surfaces of the mandible in the region of the cuspids and bicuspids (figs. 16

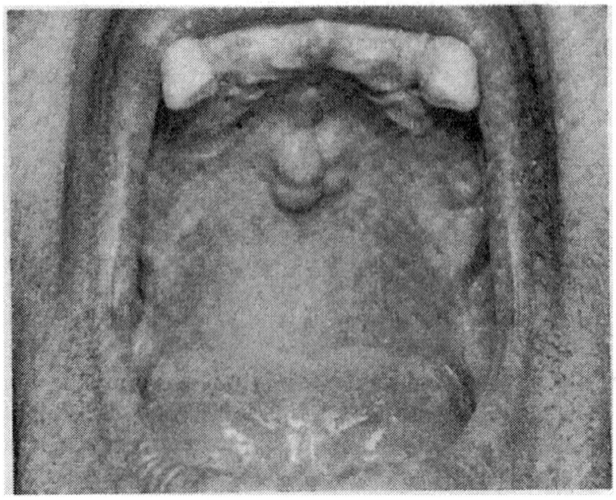

Figure 16. Torus palatinus.

and 17). They are covered with relatively thin mucosa. The names torus palatinus and torus mandibularis indicate the location of these benign bulges of excess bone. Tori develop slowly and do not require removal unless they interfere with speech, denture design, or are repeatedly irritated during normal mastication.

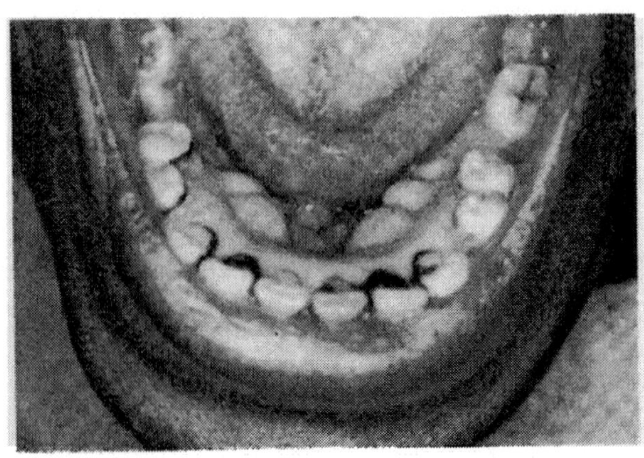

Figure 17. Torus mandibularis.

Section VIII. ABNORMALITIES AND DISEASES OF THE TONGUE

53. General

The tongue may be affected by most oral soft tissue lesions, but certain lesions are peculiar to the tongue. These lesions may be the result of developmental anomalies, systemic disorders, local irritations, or neoplastic changes. Due to the high degree of malignancy of cancers of the tongue, a thorough examination must be made to insure early discovery of these lesions which would otherwise be overlooked.

54. Developmental Abnormalities

a. Median Rhomboid Glossitis. This lesion generally appears as irregular, tumor-like elevations on which filiform papillae do not develop. However, it may develop as a midline depression with small nodular masses in the deeper areas. The lesion is benign and requires no treatment unless an irregular depression occurs, in which proper cleansing of the area by the patient constitutes treatment.

b. Cleft or Bifid Tongue. This lesion is characterized by the failure of the two halves of the tongue to unite. It occurs rarely. The cleft tongue is usually normal in size but its function is greatly impaired. Treatment is surgical, if indeed indicated.

c. Partial Ankyloglossia (fig. 18). The tongue in this condition is restricted in its movements by a strand of mucosa which extends from the ventral surface of the tip of the tongue onto the lingual gingival mucosa. This commonly called tonguetie.

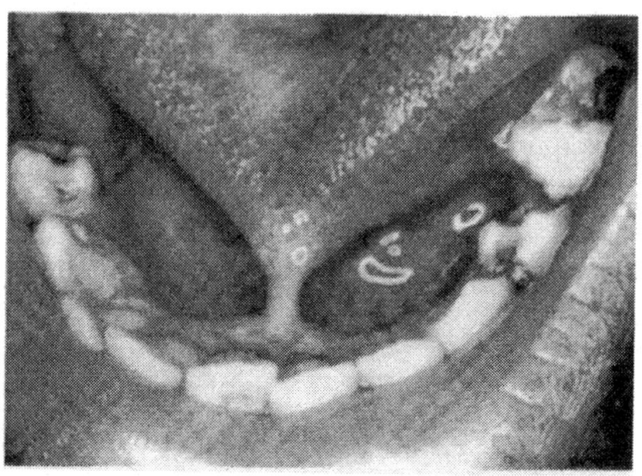

Figure 18. Ankyloglossia.

d. Fissured (Scrotal) Tongue. The surface of the tongue appears furrowed with a deep median fissure and numerous shorter fissures radiating out on either side or seen as independent furrows. This condition is usually painless. However, with food accumulation pain may result; therefore, proper cleansing of the tongue is essential.

e. Aglossia. This is a developmental anomaly in which a portion or all of the tongue is absent. Rarely is all the tongue absent.

f. Geographic Tongue. Geographic tongue (fig. 19) is characterized by alternating red areas bordered by yellowish-white. This appearance is due to alternating areas of hypertrophy and atrophy of the filiform papillae. In the zones of atrophy, the fungiform papilla appear as irregular reddish areas surrounded by keratosis. The cause of this lesion is unknown and the patterns developed are variable with changes in shape and position from time to time. Developmental defects may also be present which are responsible, due to debris collection, for a secondary burning sensation. Treatment consists of proper cleansing of the tongue.

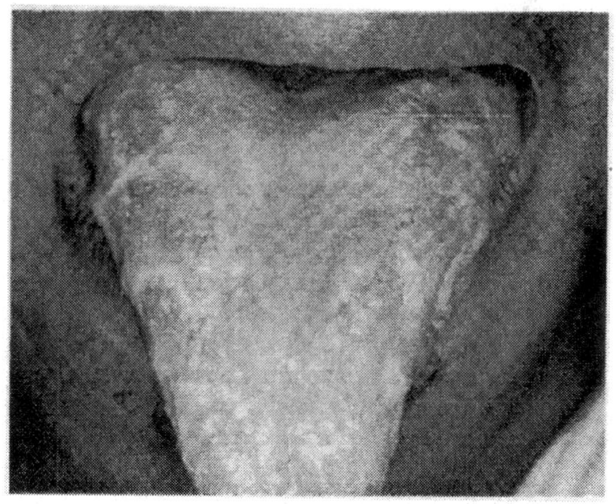

Figure 19. Geographic tongue.

g. Macroglossia. A congenital macroglossia is generally caused by an overdevelopment of the muscular portion of the tongue. Treatment is surgical correction in severe cases.

55. Black Hairy Tongue

In black hairy tongue, a local irritation, the only portion of the tongue usually affected is the dorsum just anterior to the circumvallate papillae. Accumulations of debris in the area of the filiform papillae cause this condition. The "hairs" observed are hyperkeratinized, hyperplastic filiform papillae that are secondarily discolored. Clinically, the color of the tongue ranges from yellow to brownish-yellow to black. Treatment is good oral hygiene and cleansing of the tongue.

56. Systemic Disorder (Smooth Tongue)

This disorder, smooth tongue, is also known as beefy or bald tongue of Sandwith. The bright, "beefy" red tongue is associated with pernicious anemia, pellagra, or nicotinic acid deficiency. The smoothness is caused by the atrophy of the papillae. Riboflavin deficiency may cause a magenta-colored atrophic tongue.

Section IX. DEVELOPMENTAL ANOMALIES OF THE TEETH

57. General

Anomalies are marked deviations from the normal standards as evidenced by alterations in color, contour, size, and rate or lack of development of the teeth. Systemic as well as local factors may operate to affect the presence or absence of the form or the structure of the teeth. Such influences may begin before or after birth so that either deciduous or permanent teeth may be involved. More often it is the permanent teeth which are influenced and, in all instances, only those not completely formed at the time of the disturbance.

58. Hypoplasia

In hypoplasia there is a lack of development or a defective development of the tooth before its eruption. Enamel hypoplasia in deciduous teeth can be caused by a disturbance in the enamel formation before birth and for some deciduous teeth, after birth. For permanent teeth, enamel hypoplasia can only be caused by some disturbance after birth as enamel formation of the permanent dentition begins at birth. Enamel prisms are deposited by the enamel organ in a definite pattern to form the crown of the tooth. A local disturbance may interfere with this process and result in defective development. The degree of the defect (hypoplasia) varies from mild, shallow depressions or grooves to extensive grooves or pits arranged in horizontal rows around the crown extending into the enamel as far as the dentino-enamel junction, to a lack of development of all or part of the enamel leaving exposed dentin. Hypoplastic enamel and poorly formed dentin can be attributed to various causes or combinations of them, such as infectious diseases (scarlet fever, measles, pneumonia), rickets, endocrine disturbances (parathyroids, pituitary thyroid), nutritional deficiencies (deficiencies of vitamin A, vitamin D, vitamin C, calcium, or phosphorus), or fluorosis (excess fluoride). Treatment is based on prevention with careful and systematic health supervision including proper treatment of infant diseases, good nutrition and sunshine and fresh air.

59. Anodontia

Anodontia, which means absence of teeth, is an anomaly in which the enamel organ fails to form. Some (partial anodontia) or all (total anodontia) of the teeth may fail to form. Cases in which only part of the tooth fails to form are considered forms of hypoplasia.

60. Mottled Enamel (Dental Fluorosis) (fig. 20)

Mottled enamel is a form of enamel hypoplasia which results from the ingestion of excessive fluoride during the period of enamel formation. To cause mottling, fluoride must be present in concentrations several times that found in controlled fluoridated water supplies. The mottling of enamel varies in extent and severity, depending on the amount of fluoride in the water and how long it was routinely used. In mild cases, the enamel is opaque but of good structure; in severe cases, it may be chalky and crumble easily. The area of involvement varies from spots on a few teeth to extensive mottling of many teeth. The mottled areas may have a white, opaque appearance, or they may have a stained appearance ranging from yellowish to dark brown. Because of the latter color the condition is often

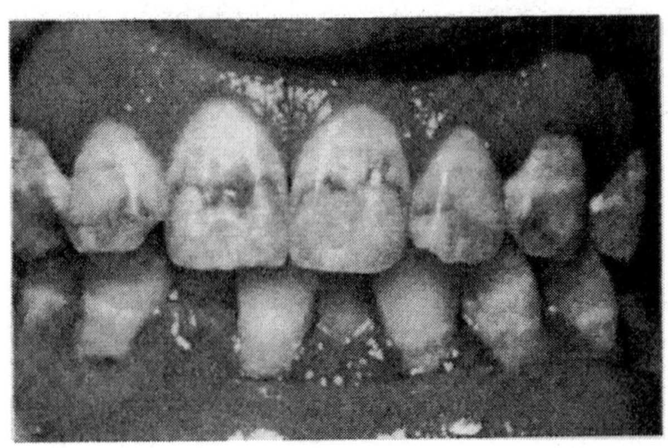

Figure 20. Mottled enamel.

referred to as "brown stain." The disease is significant mainly because it makes teeth unsightly.

61. Hypocalcification

The defective development of the enamel matrix may cause a condition called hypocalcification, which results from mineral deficiency. Hypocalcification appears as one or more small whitish spots on the tooth surface.

62. Hereditary Amelogenesis Imperfecta (Enamel Agenesis)

Enamel agenesis is a hereditary condition which involves a generalized disturbance of the enamel forming cells (ameloblasts). The teeth are generally pitted, discolored, and unsightly.

63. Hereditary Dentinogenesis Imperfecta (Opalescent Dentin)

In the condition called opalescent dentin, the teeth have a discolored glossy appearance due to progressive changes in the dentin.

64. Hyperplasia

In hyperplasia there is an abnormal multiplication or increase of the normal cells in normal arrangement in a tissue. In dental hyperplasia there may be additional enamel organs which form predeciduous teeth and postpermanent teeth (or an incomplete third dentition). There may also be supernumerary teeth (those formed beyond the conventional number). Supernumerary cusps or roots may develop on otherwise normal or supernumerary teeth.

65. Other Developmental Abnormalities

a. Dens in Dente. This is the condition in which, during the developmental state, a tooth within a tooth is formed, usually of enamel, sometimes including dentin and cementum.

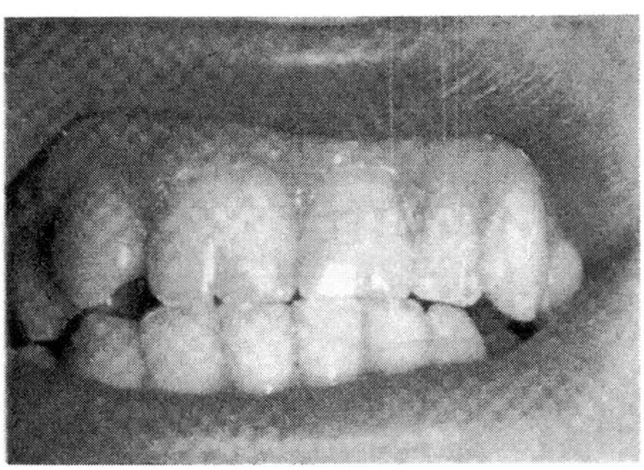

Figure 21. Fusion of maxillary central and lateral incisors.

b. Concrescence. In this condition, after the roots are developed, cementum is deposited between two adjoining teeth, joining them together. Only the roots are united. The crowns are always separate. The cause of concrescence is unknown.

c. Fusion. Fusion may occur between two normal adjoining teeth (fig. 21) or between a normal tooth and a supernumerary. Fusion may involve the crown and root (total fusion) or the roots may be separate. Usually there are two distinct pulp chambers. In fusion of the root the dentin of the two teeth is continuous as opposed to concrescence.

d. Gemination. Gemination or twin formation (fig. 22) is the condition in which a double crown is attached to a single root. The crown appears twice as wide as normal with a shallow groove through the center.

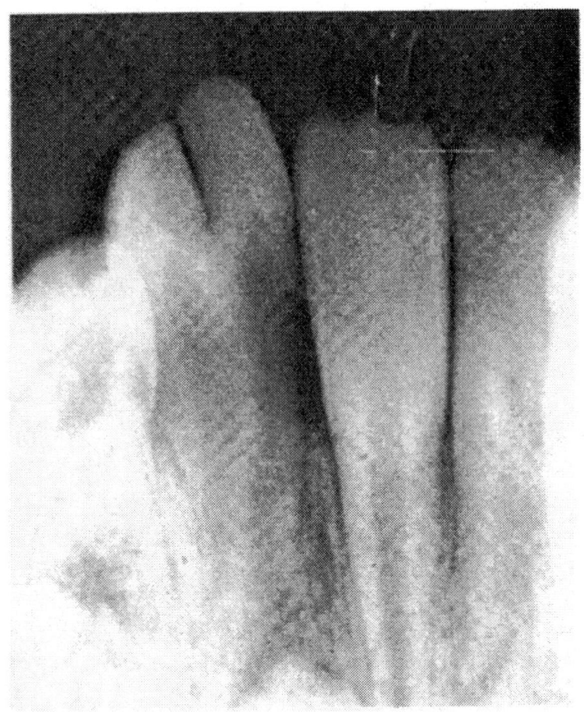

Figure 22. Gemination of mandibular anterior tooth.

e. Enamel Pearls (Enamel Drops). These are small (microscopic to 1 to 2 mm in diameter) islands of enamel located on the root surface close to the cementoenamel junction. If covered by cementum they probably will not be noticed on the extracted tooth except histologically.

Section X. FRACTURES AND DISLOCATION OF THE JAWS

66. General

Fractures and dislocation of the jaws occur frequently among members of the military population, particularly in combat. Immediate treatment involves maintenance of respiration, control of hemorrhage and shock, and observation for possible brain injury. Among the more common traumatic injuries are fractures of the mandible and maxillae.

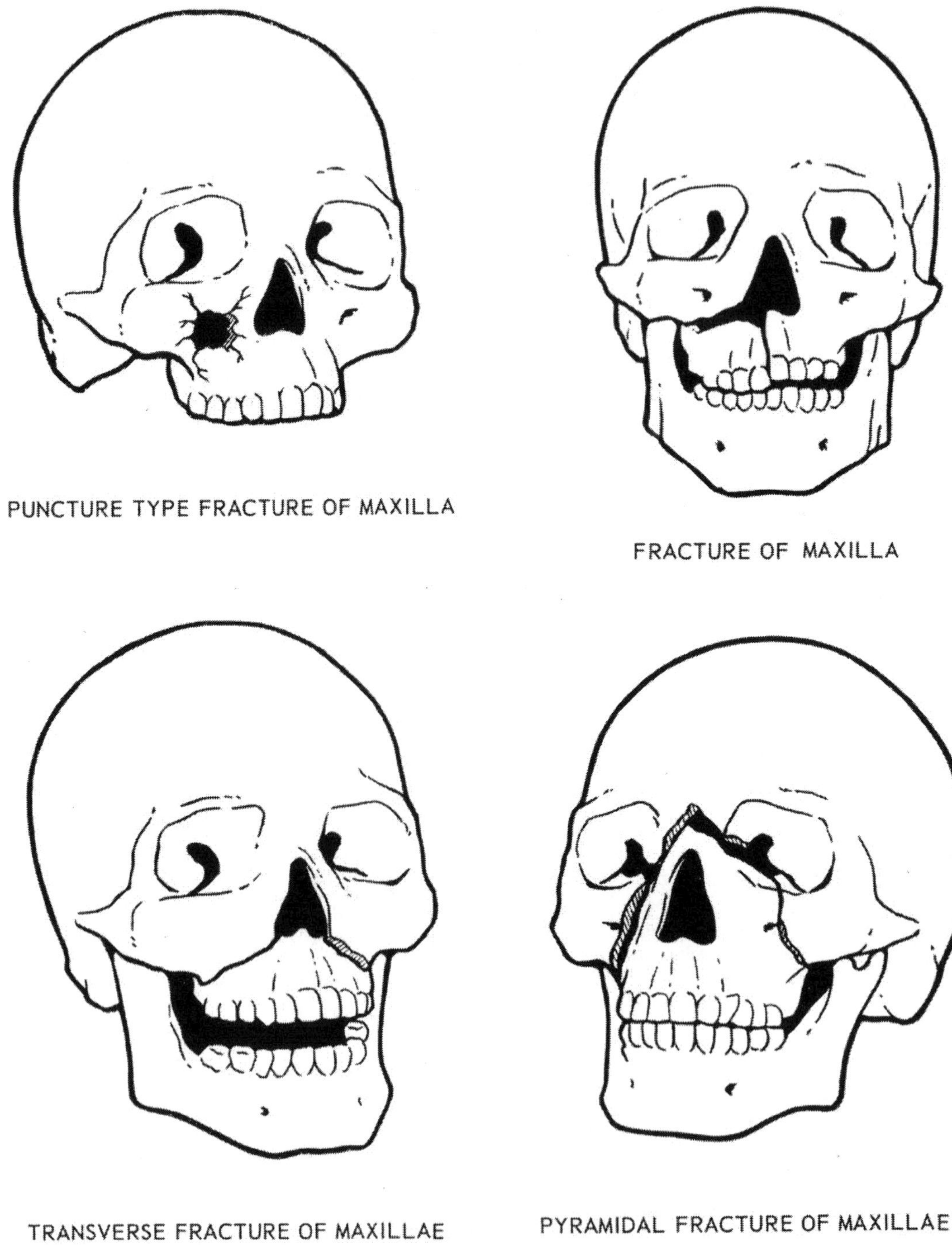

Figure .-23 (1). Fractures of the maxillae.

These fractures are often associated with varying degrees of soft tissue injury or loss, loss of bone, and comminuted or impacted fragments of bone. Such injuries are referred to the dental officer for treatment.

67. Classification of Fractures

Fractures may be classified by their severity and tissue involvement as follows:

a. Simple Fracture. A simple fracture is a break in the bone which does not produce an open wound in the skin. A simple fracture can be complete (complete severance of the bone) or incomplete. Tissue adjacent to the fracture may or may not suffer considerable injury.

b. Compound Fracture. A compound fracture is a break in the bone with an external wound leading to it.

c. Comminuted Fracture. A comminuted fracture is one in which the bone is splintered into three or more fragments or is crushed.

d. Depressed Fracture. A depressed fracture is one

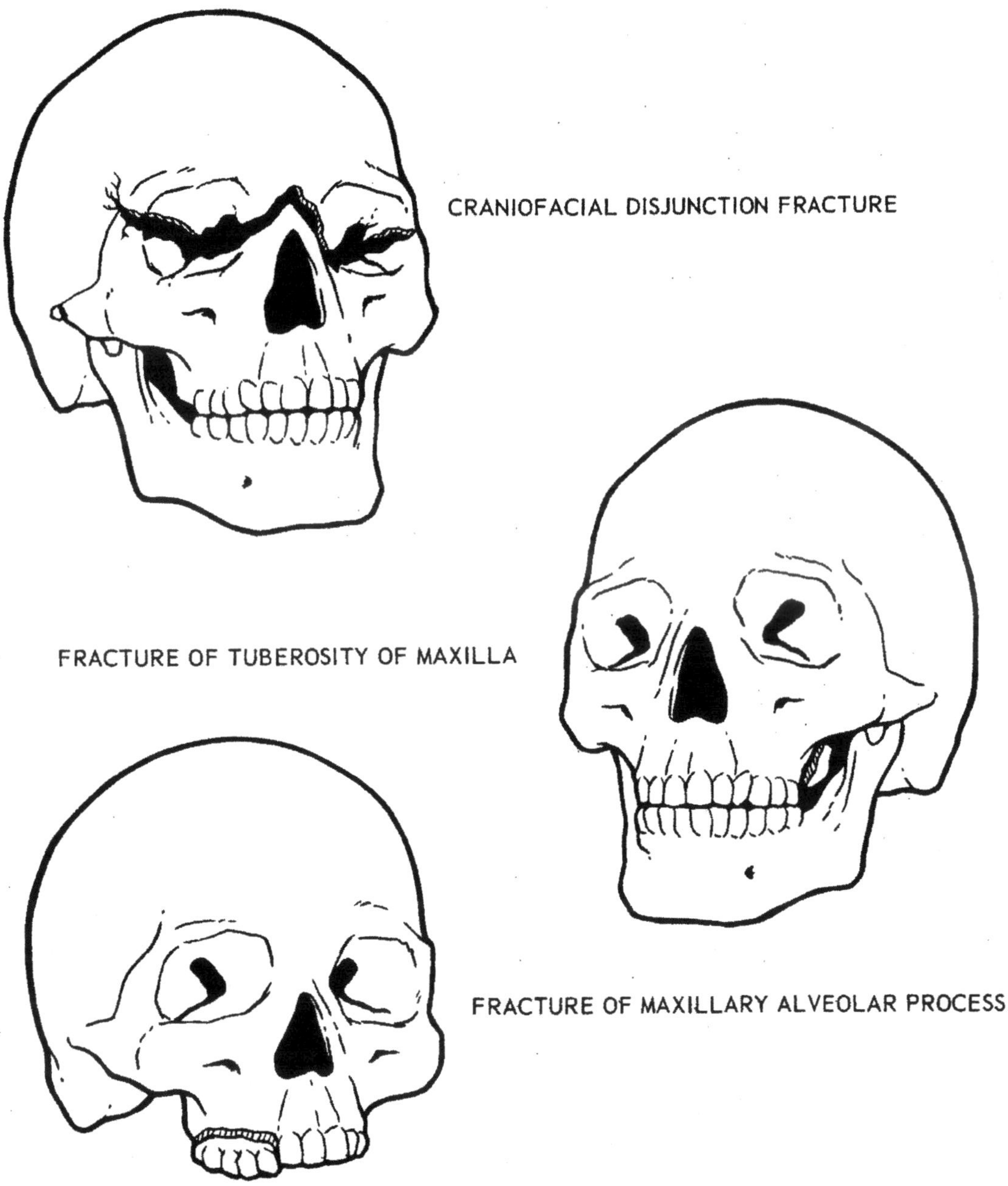

Figure 23(2). Fractures of the maxillae.

in which the fractured part is driven below the normal level of the bone, as in a skull fracture.

e. Impacted Fracture. This fracture is a break in the bone in which the hard cortical bone of one fragment is driven into the softer cancellous bone of another fragment.

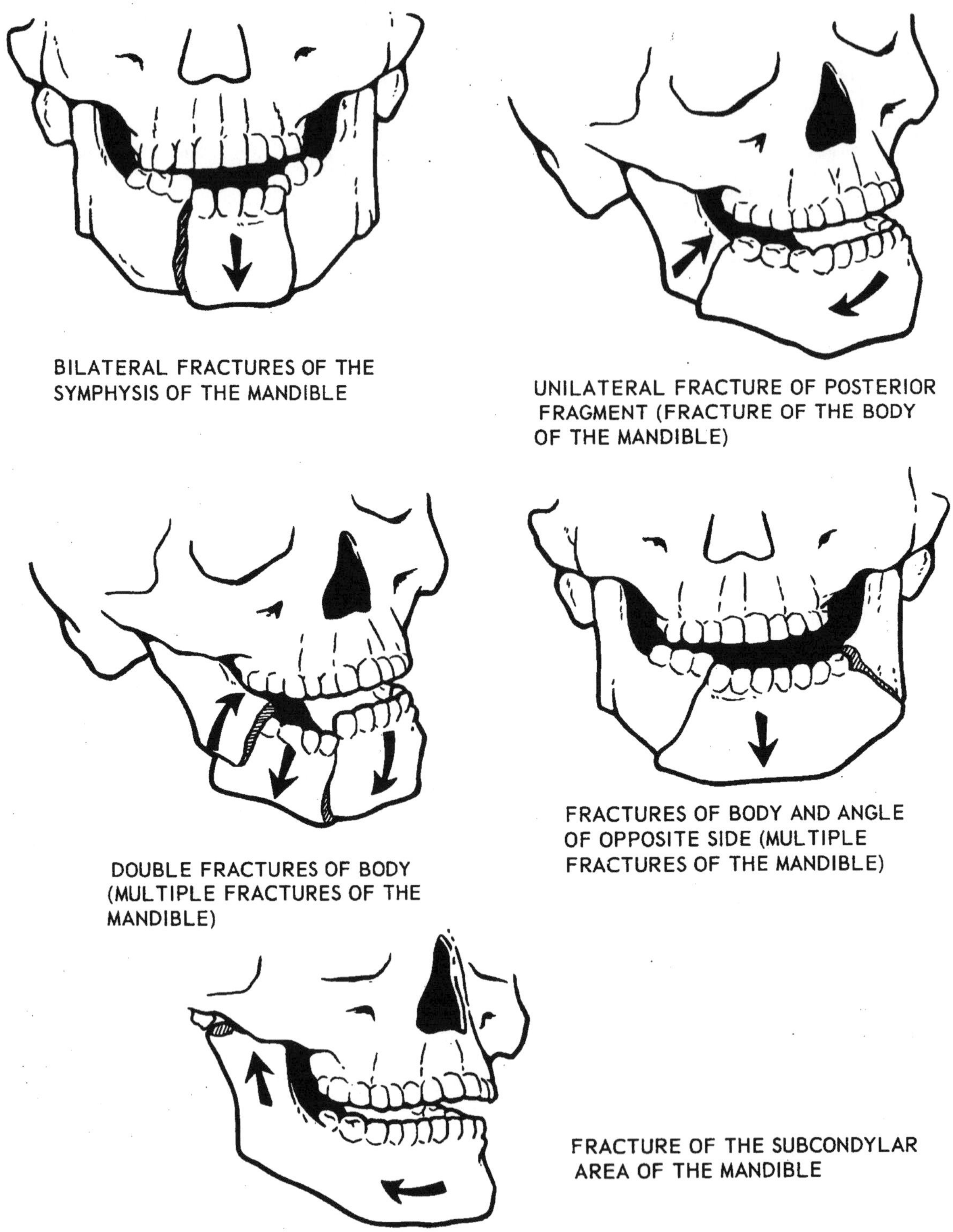

Figure 24①. Fractures of the mandible.

f. Pathologic (Spontaneous) Fracture. This fracture occurs without external violence at an area of the bone which has been weakened by a local disease.

g. Multiple Fracture. When two or more fractures occur in the same or different bones they are termed a multiple fracture.

68. Types of Jaw Fractures

(figs. 23 and 24)

a. Fractures of the maxillae include horizontal fractures through the floor of the nose, horizontal fractures of the premaxillary area, tuberosity fractures, alveolar process fractures, and nasal process fractures.

b. Fractures of the zygomatic bone include fractures involving the body as well as the temporal, maxillary, and frontal processes.

c. Common sites of fractures of the mandible include the body of the mandible, the neck of the condyle, the coronoid process, and the angle of the mandible.

69. Dislocation of the Mandible

In a dislocation of the mandible, the head of the condyle is displaced from its normal relationship

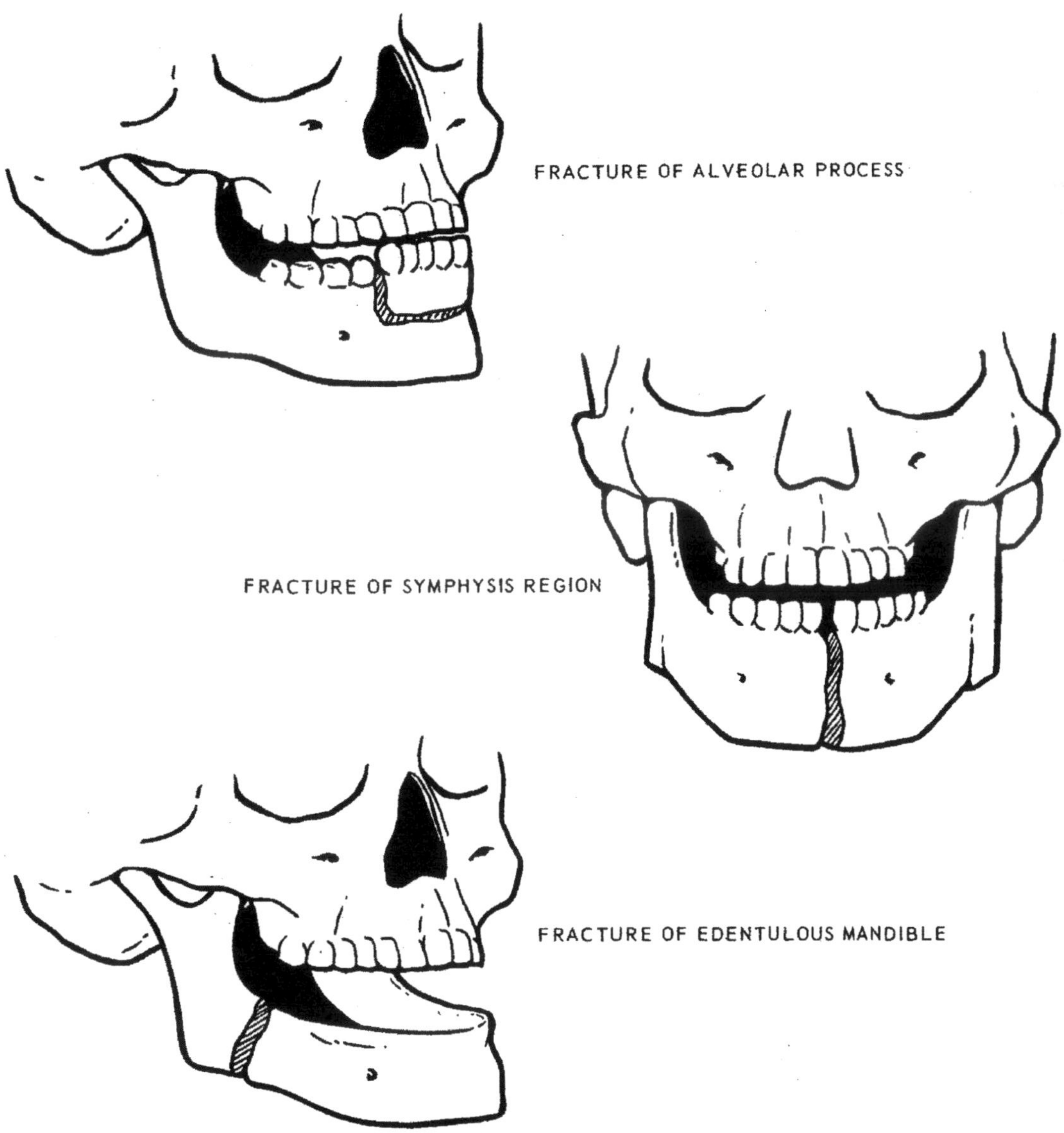

Figure 24②. Fractures of the mandible.

with the mandibular fossa; the condylar head slips down and out of the mandibular fossa, and in front of the articular tubercle. The patient is unable to close his mouth and often there is pain, discomfort, and swelling. Dislocation of the jaws may be caused by a blow, by yawning, by laughing excessively, or by otherwise opening the mouth too wide. In all cases the dental officer should be summoned immediately, for it is essential to restore the joint to its normal position. This is done by placing the thumbs in the posterior sulcus of the mandible in the region of the molar teeth and pressing downward and backward to slip the condyle under the articular tubercle. Since the jaw is likely to slip back into place quickly, it is essential to prevent the anterior teeth from being traumatically fractured.

70. Treatment of Fractures

Treatment of fractures requires restoration of the parts to their normal positions (reduction of a fracture), fixation (immobilization) of the arts for about 6 to 8 weeks until a union between the bony parts takes place. Careful postoperative care and observation are needed. Patient instruction in diet is essential because generally the teeth are immobilized in the closed position.

Section XI. ORAL MANIFESTATIONS OF SYSTEMIC DISEASE

71. General

Many systemic diseases may develop manifestations in the oral cavity, sometimes before it is evident in any other part of the body.

72. Measles

Three to 4 days before the appearance of the skin eruptions which are characteristic of measles, patches called "Koplik's spots" may appear in the oral cavity. These patches are small, irregular in shape, red, with bluish-white specks, and located on the mucosa of the cheeks and lips.

73. Mumps

Mumps is an inflammation and swelling of the parotid gland and sometimes of the submandibular gland, accompanied by headaches, chills, fever, and a swelling of the neck and cheek. The swelling usually starts below the lobe of the ear and involves the area of the parotid gland in a diffuse swelling mostly anterior to the ear. Usually there is pain when the patient attempts to open his mouth. Other parts of the body are often affected, especially in adult patients.

74. Diabetes Mellitus

Diabetes mellitus is a disease in which the body is unable to use carbohydrates (primarily sugar) due to a deficiency in the insulin secretion of the pancreas. This disease is controlled by strict dietary restriction, supplemented, as needed, by insulin or other drugs. This disease may be accompanied by dryness of the mouth, a tendency of gingival tissues to bleed easily, heavy deposits of calculus form resulting from neglect of oral hygiene, and alveolar bone loss due to the irritation of the heavy deposits of calculus.

75. Pernicious Anemia

Pernicious anemia is caused by a deficiency in the quality of hemoglobin of the blood and diminished red cell counts. Oral manifestations of this disease may be a burning sensation or numbness, a smooth, bright-red appearance of the tongue, and very pale appearance of the oral mucosa with a definite predisposition to infection and ulceration.

76. Leukemias

Leukemias are a group of fatal diseases which may show early oral symptoms. Their cause is unknown. They are characterized by marked increases in the number of leukocytes, many of which do not mature. Leukemia may vary from acute to chronic, with the acute form being more common in young persons and the chronic form in other persons. Oral symptoms include hemorrhage, ulceration, enlargement, spongy texture, and magenta coloration of the gingiva. Enlargement of lymph nodes, symptoms of anemia, and hemorrhagic tendencies are also typical. The disease occurs in myelogenous, lymphatic, and monocytic forms, each named from the type of associated predominant white blood cell.

77. Addison's Disease

With this disease there is increased deposits of melanin in the tissue. Pigmentation of the lips, mucosa, and gingiva are common. These patients are very sensitive to minor stresses, therefore, dental procedures must be carried out with proper precautions. Cause of Addison's disease is insufficient secretion of the medulla and cortex of the supra-renal glands.

78. Hemophilia

This disease of spontaneous bleeding is a sex-linked

hereditary disease confined mainly to males but transmitted through females. Spontaneous bleeding from the gingiva may occur. The eruption of teeth or extraction or exfoliation of teeth may be accompanied by hemorrhages lasting days. Since no cure is available for hemophilia, recognition of it is important before even minor dental procedures are attempted.

79. Epilepsy

This disease is discussed here because of the use of Dilantin in its treatment and the marked gingival hyperplasia that may result. In advanced hyperplasia, the teeth may be completely covered by firm, light pink gingival tissue. Normally, bleeding, inflammation or secondary infection is not a problem in these cases. Treatment of the hyperplastic tissue is surgical removal and strict oral hygiene care to prevent recurrence.

80. Tuberculosis

Tuberculosis lesions of the oral mucosa occur if wounds or erosions become infected by tubercle bacilli contained in the sputum. The oral lesions vary greatly in their appearance. The tongue is the most frequent site of the lesions. Antibiotics have been used successfully in treatment of certain types of tuberculosis.

81. Scurvy

Scurvy is a rare condition due to a deficiency of vitamin C in the diet and is marked by anemia, spongy gums, and a tendency for bleeding of the mucous tissues. The gingiva may have a purplish color.

Section XII. ORAL TUMORS (NEOPLASMS) AND LABORATORY STUDIES

82. General

A tumor is an abnormal growth of new tissue which grows independently of surrounding structures and serves no physiologic purpose. A benign tumor such as a fibroma (fig. 5-25) often is separated from the

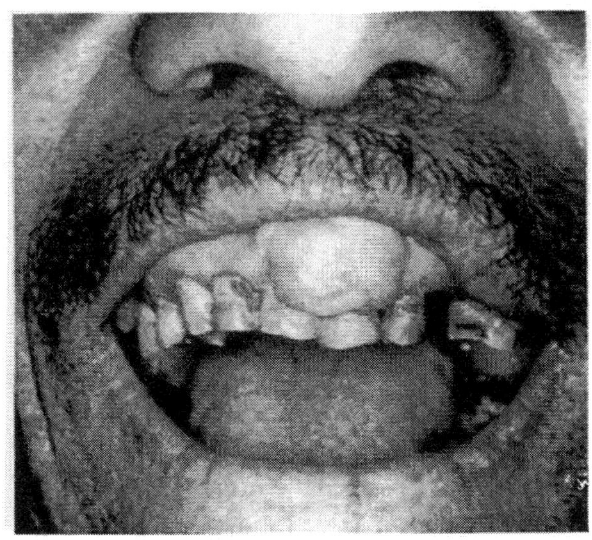

Figure 25. Fibroma.

surrounding tissues by a capsule and can usually be removed surgically. Benign tumors grow by expansion and when removed are less likely to recur than malignant tumors. Malignant tumors (cancers) gro by extension into the surrounding contiguous tissues

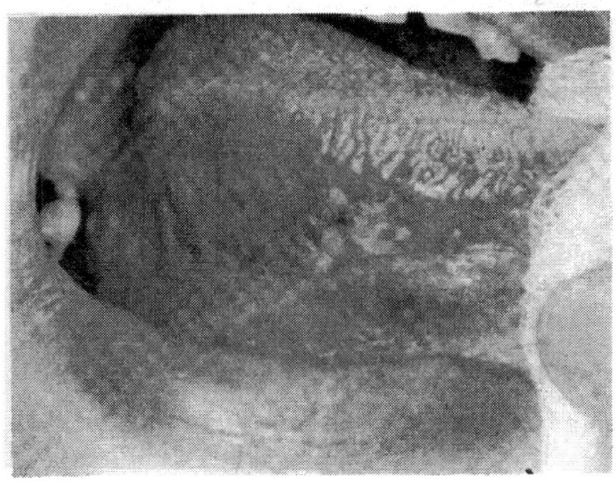

Figure 26. Early carcinoma of the tongue.

and tend to metastasize, that is, to spread to other parts of the body by the blood and lymphatic vessels. Oral cancers are shown in figures 26 and 27.

83. Observation of Abnormalities in the Oral Cavity

The oral cavity is a common site of many types of tumors. It is essential to the success of treatment of tumors to begin the treatment early. In his examination and diagnosis of oral conditions the dental officer must include a consideration of suspicious lesions such as leukoplakia or conditions which might develop into tumors. It is a responsibility of the oral hygienist to report to the dental officer any

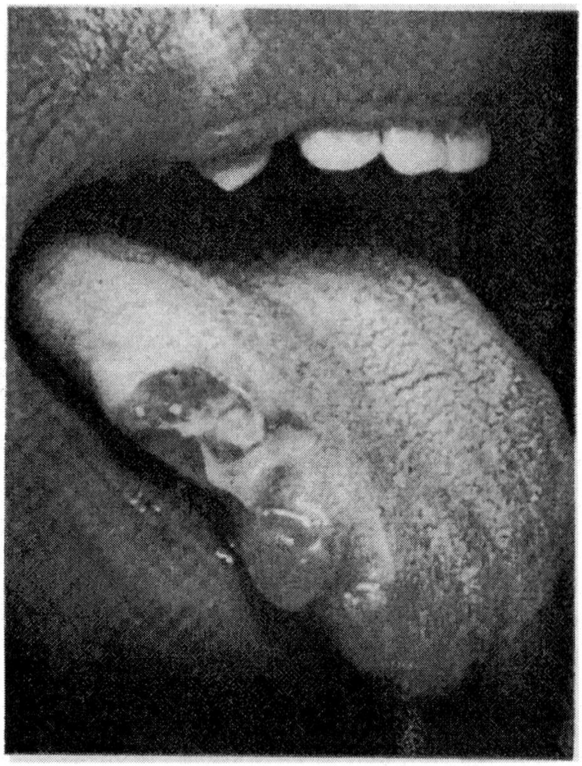

Figure 27. Advanced carcinoma of the tongue.

condition seen in the tissues of the mouth which appears abnormal whether it is an unexplained swelling, an abnormal discoloration, or an ulceration (fig. 28).

84. Biopsy

a. General. When tissue growth cannot be diagnosed by clinical observation, the dental officer may decide to obtain a tissue specimen for microscopic examination. The procedure for obtaining a tissue specimen is called biopsy. Biopsy is extremely important in diagnosing malignant growths requiring early treatment, in identifying other conditions requiring early treatment, and in identifying other conditions requiring specific types of treatment.

b. Methods (fig. 29). Surgical excision (complete removal of involved tissues) or removal of a part of the tissue may be done. Excision is the method of choice when the lesion is small and complete removal is to be the treatment. When the tissue specimen has

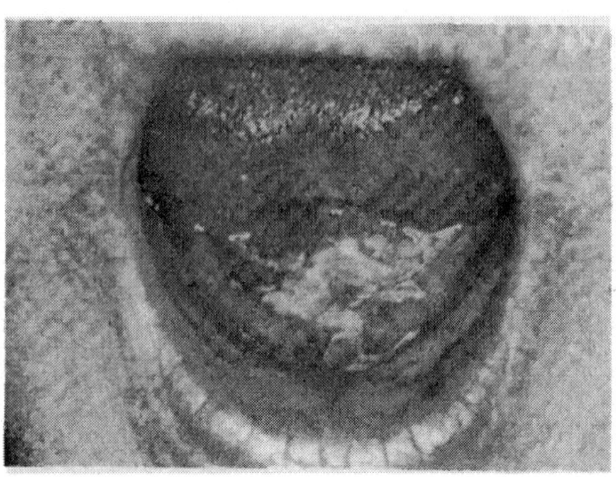

Figure 5–28. Leukoplakia.

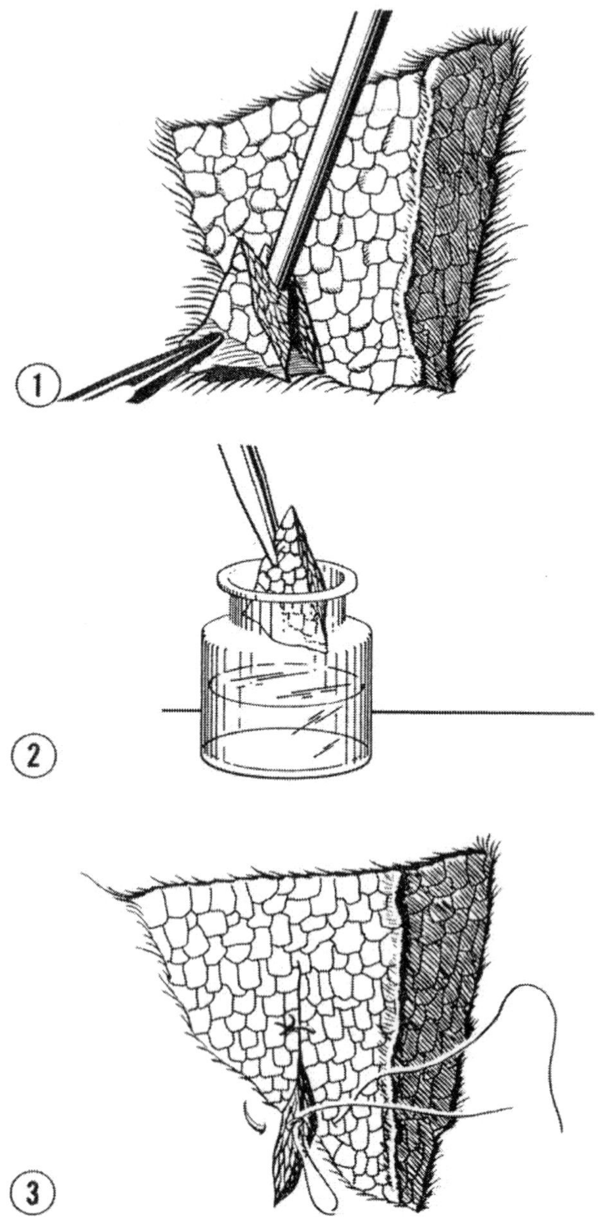

Figure 29. Biopsy techniques.

been removed surgically, it should be placed in 10 percent formalin. The bottle containing formalin should be fitted with a stopper and have an opening large enough to conveniently admit the specimen. The bottle should be large enough to contain fixative solution equal to about 20 times the volume of the specimen. Forty-eight to 72 hours is usually enough to insure adequate fixation; however, the time will be determined by the size of the specimen. The specimen-containing bottle, a properly completed Standard Form (Clinical Record–Tissue Examination), a clinical history, and appropriate dental radiograms should be forwarded to the oral pathologist.

85. Exfoliative Cytology

As a rapid screening technique, surface tissue cells can be scraped from suspicious areas, fixed, stained by the Papanicolaou technique, and studied for malignant changes. Exfoliative cytology is meant as an aid in cancer diagnosis and is not a substitute for biopsy.

Manufactured by Amazon.ca
Bolton, ON

33064777R00074